OUR BLACK COUNTRY

DAVID F. VODDEN

SUTTON PUBLISHING

Sutton Publishing Limited
Phoenix Mill · Thrupp · Stroud
Gloucestershire · GL5 2BU

First published 2003

Title page photograph: Detail of the wire machine workshop at Eyland and Sons, Lower Rushall Street, Walsall in the early 1900s.

British Library Cataloguing in Publication Data
A catalogue record for this book is available from the British Library.

ISBN 0-7509-3044-6

Typeset in 10.5/13.5 Photina.
Typesetting and origination by
Sutton Publishing Limited.
Printed and bound in England by
J.H. Haynes & Co. Ltd, Sparkford.

To my wife, Elizabeth

THE BLACK COUNTRY SOCIETY

The Black Country Society is proud to be associated with **Sutton Publishing** of Stroud. In 1994 the society was invited by Sutton Publishing to collaborate in what has proved to be a highly successful publishing partnership, namely the extension of the ***Britain in Old Photographs*** series into the Black Country. In this joint venture the Black Country Society has played an important role in establishing and developing a major contribution to the region's photographic archives by encouraging society members to compile books of photographs of the area or town in which they live.

The first book in the Black Country series was *Wednesbury in Old Photographs* by Ian Bott, launched by Lord Archer of Sandwell in November 1994. Since then 55 Black Country titles have been published. The total number of photographs contained in these books is in excess of 11,000, suggesting that the whole collection is probably the largest regional photographic survey of its type in any part of the country to date.

This voluntary society, affiliated to the Civic Trust, was founded in 1967 as a reaction to the trends of the late 1950s and early '60s. This was a time when the reorganisation of local government was seen as a threat to the identity of individual communities and when, in the name of progress and modernisation, the industrial heritage of the Black Country was in danger of being swept away.

The general aims of the society are to stimulate interest in the past, present and future of the Black Country, and to secure at regional and national levels an accurate understanding and portrayal of what constitutes the Black Country and, wherever possible, to encourage and facilitate the preservation of the Black Country's heritage.

The society, which now has over 2,500 members worldwide, organises a yearly programme of activities. There are six venues in the Black Country where evening meetings are held on a monthly basis from September to April. In the summer months, there are fortnightly guided evening walks in the Black Country and its green borderland, and there is also a full programme of excursions further afield by car. Details of all these activities are to be found on the society's website, **www.blackcountrysociety.co.uk**, and in ***The Blackcountryman***, the quarterly magazine that is distributed to all members.

PO Box 71 · Kingswinford · West Midlands DY6 9YN

CONTENTS

INTRODUCTION

One of the first questions I need to settle is 'Where is the Black Country?'. Inevitably this question is posed and the answers, particularly from Black Countrymen, vary widely. Some will say it is Cradley Heath, others that it is Gornal or that it is on the thick coal. The Black Country has been defined as being within a 3-mile radius of Dudley. Stan Hill, President of the Black Country Society, said recently, 'It is a state of mind; The Black Country is where a Black Countryman thinks it is! – within the 150 square miles, 15 miles north to south, 10 miles east to west, wherein lay the 30 foot seam of coal, iron ore and limestone.'

Elihu Burritt, American Consul in Birmingham, described the Black Country in the opening sentences of his book, *Walks in the Black Country and its Green Borderland*, in 1868 as 'black by day and red by night . . . week in week out, and often seven days to the week . . . the Sunday evening halo . . . when the church bells are ringing to service on winter nights, glows "redder than the moon".'

Describing some English immigrants who had arrived on Vancouver Island on the *Princess Royal* in November 1854, it was reported 'that they had come from England's Black Country, an industrial region in central England where most men worked in coal mines and where living conditions were less than ideal'. Some writers in the 1940s quoted the *Encyclopaedia Britannica*: 'a district of the English Midlands including South Staffordshire with parts of Worcestershire and Warwickshire. The name is due to the numerous collieries and furnaces, and the desolation of scenery and agglomeration of houses consequent upon the mining of coal, ironstone, and clay and dependent industries. The district is intersected by canals, now mostly derelict . . .', but not providing a map of the boundaries.

For my purposes I have taken the more modern definition initiated by the 1974 Local Government changes and taken up by the Government when it established the Black Country Development Corporation, identifying four Black Country Metropolitan Boroughs: Dudley, Sandwell, Walsall and Wolverhampton. Whatever place is said to be the true Black Country by partisans of their own areas, they are now within one of these four boroughs. On 21 March 1991 the *Express & Star* also bravely published a Map of the Black Country!

Phil Drabble had written as long ago as 1952 that 'the Black Country is fast becoming no more than a memory. For one thing it is no longer black.' Nevertheless, when I collected pictures for this book I found that knowledge and memories of the Black Country were both very clear in everyone's mind. Coupled with nostalgia, there is also a very strong sense of pride in the achievements of the Black Country, particularly in heavy manufacturing industry, and considerable regret at the closing of so many works belonging to firms which had become household names: Round Oak, Rubery Owen, Garringtons, F.H. Lloyd, Wellman Smith Owen, Patent Shaft and many more.

Black Countrymen and women had taken great pride in their work, hard though it was at times. They enjoyed making things, using their hands and their skills. Although conditions in the nineteenth century were sometimes severe, almost savage, the attitude of many employers in the twentieth century often became consciously benevolent towards the workforce, both during their working lives and afterwards in their retirement. The late Lord Raymond Brookes of West Bromwich was Chairman of Garringtons and, driving through Darlaston one day, saw a number of his pensioners just sitting about in the town centre. The firm already had a forty-year club for pensioners who had worked for Garringtons for forty years, so he founded another, the Evergreen Room, to provide a social base for all his other pensioners. J.A. Crabtree founded Crabtree Electrical in 1919 and, having grown up in Lancashire and seen the working conditions in the mills, vowed to provide much better for his workers when he had his own business. At its peak, Crabtree's employed upwards of 2,000 at any one time. Following his early death at forty-seven, all workers received an extra week's wages in his will. Recently, the parent company Electrium has closed down its operation in Walsall while retaining its local presence in Brownhills. There are many ex-workers who are proud to say they worked at Crabtree's where standards were very high indeed. To maintain quality, long before British Standards (BS) numbers were introduced, Crabtree's made everything, except ceramics for their switches. They even made and threaded their brass terminal screws!

As I chatted to Black Country people, while compiling the pictures for this book, I found it very heart-warming to learn of their pride in their job and their affection for the firm for whom, in many cases, they had worked for many years.

Within a very small radius of Dudley Castle, Lord Dudley established the Round Oak Iron and Steel Works in 1857, following the lead of his forebears, who operated iron and cast-iron manufactories from the seventeenth century. Dud Dudley, an illegitimate son of the family, had introduced the coking of coal to the area in the seventeenth century and operated a furnace in Dudley and two furnaces on Pensnett Chase, producing 7 tons of iron a week. The secrets of coking appeared to have died with him and did not reappear until the early eighteenth century in the hands of Dudley-born Abraham Darby in Coalbrookdale. Compared with many other landowners, Lord Dudley was a rare entrepreneur. Whereas they relied upon rents from tenant farmers and so on, he derived a large income from exploiting the minerals under his land. The Black Country had, beneath its surface, considerable deposits of coal (some of it 30ft thick), iron and clay as well as extensive limestone. Marrying these, coked coal, iron ore and limestone, formed the basis for the great iron and steel industry.

Different villages in the Black Country tended to specialise in their specific products. While Lye and Halesowen were the centres for nailmaking, Cradley Heath and, of course, Mushroom Green were the bases for chainmaking and, in the early days, it was hand-wrought chain using wrought iron. Not only men worked at this, but women too. The famous Lucy Woodhall of Old Hill worked for sixty years and one month making chain until 1973, although her childhood skill was in fine needlework!

With chain, there was also anchor forging. It is surprising how many industries situated in the heart of the country made products which were to be used at sea or, at

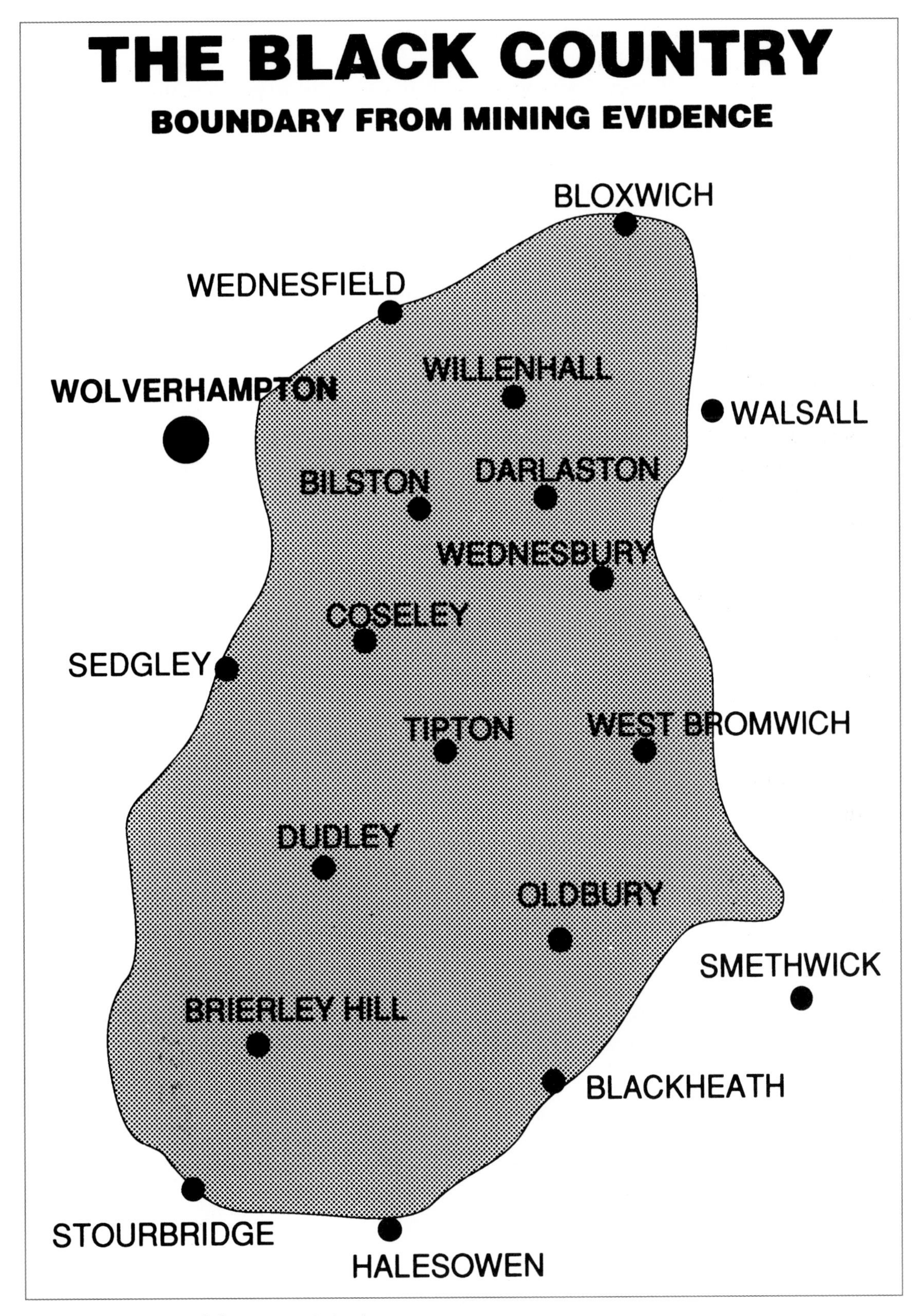

(*By kind permission of the* Express & Star)

least, exported. Hingleys of Netherton forged anchors, including those of the *Titanic* and, in that instance, had to transport them to the Harland and Wolff shipyard in Belfast. In structural engineering Rubery Owen was a leader, and gained contracts not only locally but as far afield as Wembley Stadium, Oxford Circus underground station and Ewell Technical College in Surrey. Garringtons' forges produced automotive parts in peace and munitions in war. They had sizeable contracts with both the War Office and the Admiralty. Lock making was not unique to Willenhall. James Gibbons' Locks, reputedly the oldest lock makers in the country, founded in the late seventeenth century, was based in Wolverhampton and specialised in lock systems for prisons and mental hospitals. Manders of Wolverhampton continue to manufacture paint, printing ink and now computer ink. Chances of Oldbury not only produced the glass for the Crystal Palace of the Great Exhibition but also prism lenses for lighthouses such as the Longshore and, even at Leeuwin Point, the southernmost lighthouse in the world, in Australia.

During my research I have been lucky enough to meet two men who were reponsible for completing the closure of the major works of Garringtons and Round Oak Steelworks to the extent that, in both cases, they were literally the last to leave, padlocking the gates behind them.

'This picture shows Garrington's Forging site being cleared once all manufacturing had been finished. It took me about eighteen months to close the site down with a small team of men.' (*Peter Wright*)

Rowley Rag Quarry, 1991. It is an example of the rich mineral resources of the Black Country. (*Geoff Warburton*)

Brian Stead, former chief engineer at Round Oak, recalls that the announcement of the first tranch of redundancies was made at a meeting at Chateau Impney near Droitwich in 1980 following TI's selling of their 50 per cent share to Brierley Hill Development (BSC). This reduced the workforce from 3,000 to 2,100. There were to be three tranches in total reducing the workforce to 1,250 in 1982 and, finally, at a public meeting in Dudley Town Hall on 17 November 1982 notice was given to close on Christmas Day the same year. Although there was no manufacturing after 1982, it took until 30 June 1985 to complete the closure and dispose of the equipment, leaving the buildings intact with services connected. Brian Stead recalls the lesson he learnt about market values at such times. For example, 900 office desks were auctioned for a total of £400! He locked the gates on 30 June and handed the keys to the Richardson twins a few days later in order that they might develop the Merry Hill Shopping Centre.

It was a similar story at Garringtons in Darlaston where Peter Wright headed a small team of fifty to close the works. Again, the forge hammers and other equipment went for next to nothing or were scrapped. He too was the last to leave and padlocked the gates of a factory site where, at one time, 1,100 used to work.

This book contains evidence not only of the past era of manufacturing industry, but also of the way of life of ordinary people. I hope the reader will enjoy recalling the past and share a sense of pride in the achievements of the Black Country.

David F. Vodden

1

The Black Country Boroughs

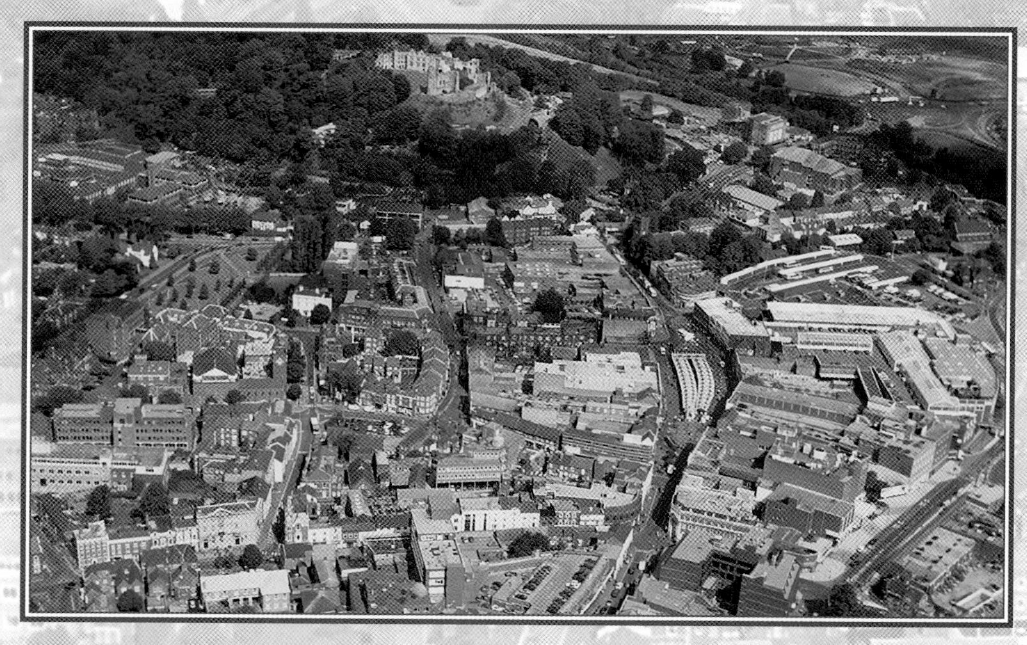

Mrs Mary Stephens says, 'Just over sixty years ago my daily journey to and from Dudley High School began. This picture by David Wilkins of Dudley from the air shows the castle ruins dominating the town and marking the beginning of the High Street, which passes "Bottom" church on the right, winding through the Market Stalls with their striped awnings to "Top" church in the centre foreground. The building in the top left section could be the former Technical College, but the High School will not be found; the site is now a Municipal car park! The Town Hall, middle left, brings back memories of speech days, "Jerusalem" and slippery steps to the platform, but immediately below, a remaining part of older Dudley; a row of Georgian buildings.' (*David Wilkins at First House Photography*)

Geoff Warburton says, 'I took this picture of Dudley Castle from 500 ft in the air in "Bustin Wendi" balloon on 22 July 1997. You can also see the Eve Hill flats to the West and Queen's Road flats to the south-west.' Elihu Burritt wrote in 1868, 'Dudley Castle needs only a pen like Sir Walter Scott's to make it famous. . . . From the Castle Hill of Dudley Nature has the underhand, and from the crown of her head to the sole of her foot she is scourged with cat-o'-nine-tails of red-hot wire, and marred and scarred and fretted, and smoked half to death day and night . . .'. (*Geoff Warburton*)

'My picture of Sedgley Beacon, 17 June 1999, when we waited for Morris Dancers, reminds us of its popularity for many years as a picnic spot and piece of countryside for visitors from the conurbation.' Phil Drabble described the view from the tower in 1952 in his book on the Black Country: 'From the parapet at the top the whole world suddenly prostrates itself. To one side, on the west, are green fields and pleasant farms – the lovely hills of Shropshire and Worcestershire. Nothing to be ashamed of there. On a clear day you can see the Wrekin and the Clees and the Clents – and all the rolling rural land between. It's the view to the other side that strangers dislike. At first glance it looks like one huge town from Wolverhampton, in the north, right over to Walsall, in the east, and round to West Bromwich. . . . A second glance shows a huge patchwork quilt. No brilliant, gaudy colours, but a sober patchwork of duns and browns, and browny-greens and slate blues, and dull reds. An intricate pattern of town mingling with country. The hillside at the base of the beacon tower is green. Bright where cattle graze and a yellower green of corn to the left. Slashed ruthlessly across this scene is a conspicuous row of electric cables, like a scar across the belly of the earth, where every pylon is a stitch. . . .

'A country scene as flat as this would have a series of village churches for landmarks. Perhaps, here and there, would be a windmill or great mansion. But the chief landmarks in the Black Country are far more prosaic. The salient points are not picturesque churches, venerable and rich in history. They are power stations.' (*Geoff Warburton*)

'I took this picture of the Tilted Barrel, Tipton, in the 1970s because it was a good example of a "pit-pulled" building, that is, it had suffered from subsidence due to coal-mining.' (*D.F. Vodden*)

'This is an early twentieth-century picture postcard of High Street, Dudley. Trams were employed in those days.' (*Geoff Warburton*)

'I took this on 12 December 1994 because the owner of Whitefriars, Church Lane, Halesowen, fought hard against its threatened demolition.' (*Geoff Warburton*)

'This is a view along Priory Street towards Dudley Castle which I took on 29 January 1989.' (*Geoff Warburton*)

'This is a view on 18 September 1991 of the sixteenth-century residential block at Dudley Castle, which had been designed by William Sharrington of Lacock Abbey. From this viewpoint at the top of the fourteenth-century Great Tower Keep, you can also see Coseley, Deepfields, Springvale and Willenhall.' (*Geoff Warburton*)

'Lord Dudley's agent, Mr Russon, lived at this address in Old King Street from 1861 and it is probably the oldest building in Netherton. I took the photograph on 24 September 1989.' (*Geoff Warburton*)

'This is a picture postcard view of Dudley Market, *c.* 1900. It shows the cast-iron public weighbridge which was to be relocated to Stane Street in the 1920s. Eventually it was saved in 1967 for the Black Country Living Museum.' (*Geoff Warburton*)

'I took this shot of Dudley from Tipton Street on 7 June 1995. You can see the Dudley Hippodrome and its huge fly tower at the back. The proposed line of the Midland Metro tramway used the South Staffs line and then climbs into Dudley by skirting the back of the Plaza Cinema at the top right of the picture.' (*Geoff Warburton*)

'I took this picture of Dudley Market on 25 May 1996, looking along the High Street towards "Top Church".' (*Geoff Warburton*)

This aerial shot of the centre of West Bromwich was taken in 2000 by David Wilkins at First House Photography. Mike Whitehouse, who has worked as an accountant for some time in West Bromwich, says, 'This is clearly taken during the middle of a working day judging by the number of cars in the multi-storey car park and a market day, too. It shows the old bus station which is to be the site of the Jubilee Arts complex. Bache's solicitors' pentagonal office building is in the centre foreground and used to have a fish pond in the middle stocked with carp. It was somewhere for workers at lunch time. The Metro line is completed at top right and B&Q is at bottom left.' (*David Wilkins at First House Photography*)

'The trams used to run from Carters Green to the boundary at Handsworth. On the corner of the Wesleyan church in this picture used to be Hansons' office.' (*Derek Pester*)

'I remember how West Bromwich Manor House used to be divided up into tenements and was surrounded by fields. It was about to be demolished when junior architect John Dryden drew Ansells' attention to its historical value. It was restored by the Birmingham City Architect Manzoroni and leased to Ansells.' (*Derek Pester*)

'The Rolfe Street Baths, Smethwick, before being dismantled prior to transfer to the Black Country Living Museum. They have now been re-erected to provide large exhibition halls and archive storage.' (*D.F. Vodden*)

'This shows the former Rolfe Street Baths from Smethwick re-erected at the Black Country Museum, 2000.' (*Ron Julian*)

This view of Walsall from the air was taken by David Wilkins in 2000. It looks along Wolverhampton Street towards the rear of the new Woolworths store and the Walsall New Art Gallery. It is on one of the five market days and Park Street is paved in red brick nowadays. In the left foreground either side of Shaw Street, the construction of the new up-market retail area is underway. (*David Wilkins at First House Photography*)

'I took this picture of the former Wharfinger's cottage by the Town Wharf, Walsall, in 1994 while it was still dilapidated. It has now been restored.' (*D.F. Vodden*)

'I had lovely memories of Saturday matinees at the former Savoy Cinema which I photographed being demolished. It originally had a single auditorium with a nice big screen which I particularly liked, which for me was reminiscent of the Odeon, Leicester Square! It was amazing how strongly it was built and it took some time to demolish.' (*Gordon Hill*)

Gordon Hill lectures at Walcat. 'I used to pop out to watch Woolworths being built on the site of the former cinema. I thought it was an interesting building and had seen the architect's model for the whole Town Wharf development. I understand that its design was influenced by the shape of Her Majesty's Theatre which had stood there in 1900.' (*Gordon Hill*)

Retired architect Rob Madeley says, 'I took this over forty years ago in High Street, Walsall. In those days they took the market stalls down as there were only two markets a week. As a result, people could park their cars up and down the High Street. For a time I was Honorary Secretary of the Walsall Civic Society which worked hard to maintain the town's heritage.' (*R.G. Madeley*)

'I am confident that this view of Walsall High Street from the steps of St Matthew's Church was taken in about 1900 by keen amateur photographer Arthur Farrington, who was to become President of Walsall Photographic Society in 1953 at the age of seventy-two.' (*John Griffiths*)

'Highgate Windmill is situated only a few metres away from the site of Hope Cottage, which was the family home of the Eylands who owned a bucklemaking factory in Lower Rushall Street.' (*John Griffiths*)

'This picture of the official opening of the Co-op Dairy, Midland Road, Walsall on 10 July 1937 was taken by H.C. Herbert of the *Walsall Times & South Stafford Advertiser.* Mr Thomas Gwinnett, President of the Society, is addressing the 500 members who attended the ceremony. In the background are three buildings familiar to generations of Walsall people: in the top left-hand corner, the out-patients department of the now-demolished General Hospital and in the opposite corner is the Congregational church. In the centre, behind the trees, is the roof of the Particular Baptist chapel.' (*John Griffiths*)

'Hope Cottage was the Eylands' family home in Highgate, Walsall from 1904 until being demolished in about 1981 to be replaced by flats.' (*John Griffiths*)

'This is a picture postcard of King Street, Darlaston as it was in the 1950s but not posted until 1970!' (*Mrs Mary Harper*)

I took these two views of Darlaston, Pinfold Street, 2002, looking west and east, because there are plans to redevelop the area. (*D.F. Vodden*)

'This picture of the Darlaston Bullstake and King Street seems to have been taken in the 1950s. On the left, the car is parked outside Appleyard's drapers. The site of their shop is now occupied by the library, opened 1987. Nearby, Asda have just built a new supermarket, opened 18 November 2002.' (*D.F. Vodden*)

David Wilkins says, 'I took this picture of the centre of Wolverhampton from the air in 1983. St Peter's parish church is clearly visible as is the Wolverhampton Wanderers' Molyneux Ground.' Dr Geoff Allman remembers the John Ireland Stand, named after a former director, at the top right-hand corner being built at great expense between 1980 and 1982. The cost led to the club's bankruptcy and it slipped to the Second Division and later the Fourth Division, largely because of the sale of players. Offices at the stand were rented by the polytechnic. (*David Wilkins at First House Photography*)

'This view of the centre of the city of Wolverhampton was taken from the air in 2002 and, compared with that of 1983, shows some changes at the Molineux Ground, with the addition of the Jack Harris Stand on the south, the Stan Cullis on the north or Bushbury end and the Billy Wright Stand on the left on the site of the old Waterloo Road Stand. The former polytechnic, now a university, has also added some buildings. The parish church of St Peter's remains largely unchanged as do the shopping streets in the lower part of the picture.' (*David Wilkins at First House Photography*)

'This picture shows posters on a wall near St Peter's Church, Wolverhampton, 1906, and reminds us of the commodities available at that time.' (*John Griffiths*)

2

The World of Work

'The District Ironworks, Birchills. My grandad was A. Etheridge who is seventh from the left in the back row and who lived in Dalkeith Street, Birchills. This was probably taken soon after the First World War. Back row, left to right: -?-, J. Reynolds, S. Haynes, J. Willey, T. Webster, J. Abnett, A. Etherington, F. Peakman, H. Guest, A. Willey, E. Willey, A. Wainwright, D. ?. Middle row: -?-, W. Parker, A. Read, W. Hill, F. Clark, N. Marsh, E. Arblaster (jnr), R. Tolley, W. Arblaster, E. Arblaster, A. ?. Front row: H. Mason, R. Bonser, W. Hands, J. Jackson, A.W. Lester, E. Arblaster (snr) C. Hands, J. Wassell, F. ?' (*Mrs E. Dwyer*)

'This is a group of workers at Bloxwich Lock & Stamping one Christmas in the early 1970s. I think that second from the left in the back row is Ruth Whitehouse, the man in the middle of that row is Jeff Roadway, on his left are Iris Cartridge and Joan Gilbert. In the front on the left is Steven Powell (Quality Inspector), Betty Heminsley, Joan Edwards, -?-, Eileen Edwards, Margaret Heminsley, Stella Dennant (née Quinn), Janet Pavlovitch, -?-.' (*Mrs B. Hemmingsley*)

These two pictures are of a group of girls who worked for the Bloxwich Lock and Stamping Co. They were taken in about 1973 in J Dept Press shop in very happy days which we will never see again. My wife did forty years and I did thirty-five years there.'

In the left-hand picture are Mrs Janet Pavlovich, Mrs Lil Thacker, Mrs Ann Hill, Mrs Betty Millward and Mrs Brenda Picken. In the right-hand picture are, left to right, Mrs Lil Thacker, Mrs Barbara Blewer, Mrs Betty Millward, Mrs Dot North and Miss Renny Arrowsmith. (*R. Millward*)

'This is the Longshore Lighthouse lens on display at the Birmingham Museum of Science and Industry, Newhall Street, 3 March 1993. It was made by Chance Brothers Ltd of Smethwick in 1826. Grace Darling (1815–42) lived in that lighthouse and became a rescue heroine in 1838. The lens is now on display at Thinktank at Millennium Point. (*Geoff Warburton*)

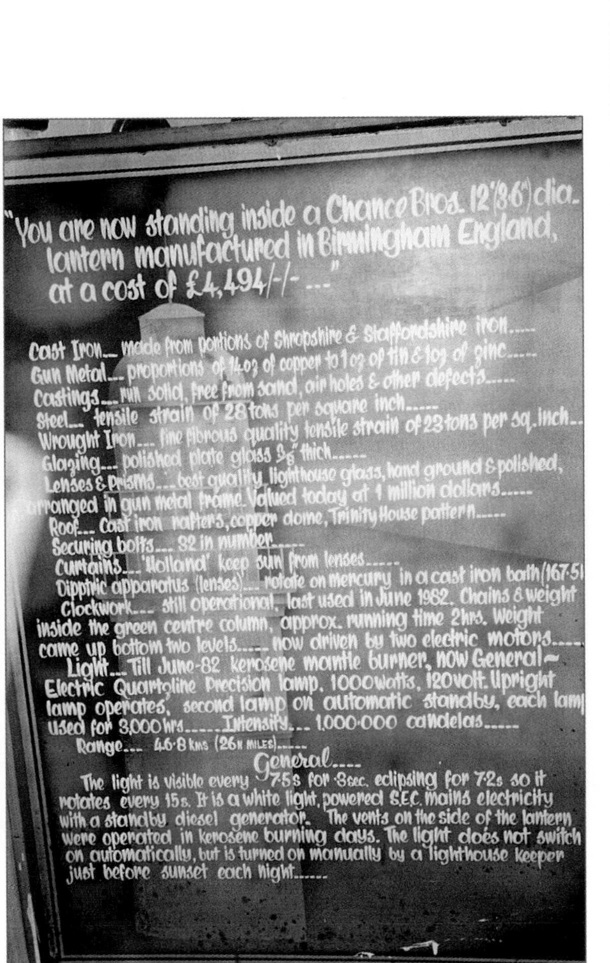

'The lighthouse at Cape Leeuwin, south-west Australia, was built in 1895 after several shipwrecks in that vicinity. The Cape was named after a Dutch captain's ship in 1622. Mapping of the Australian coastline was started here by Matthew Flinders in 1851. It is said from the top of the lighthouse you are halfway between the Equator and the Antarctic coastline. The plaque shows that the lenses were made by Chances of England (meaning Smethwick and Oldbury)'. (*I.G. Mitchell*)

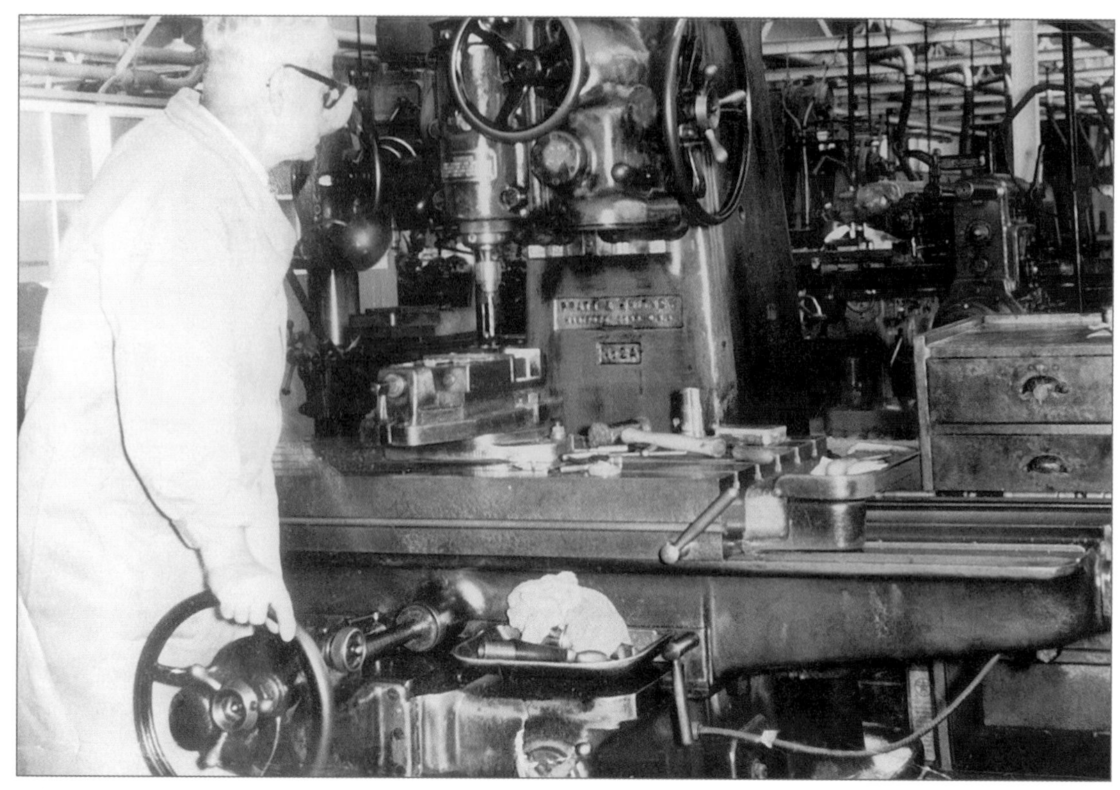

'This is my father Albert E. Jeffrey at his milling machine in J.A. Crabtree's. It sometimes took him twelve months to produce a machine tool.' (*Ken Jeffrey*)

'My father Albert E. Jeffrey with a lathe at J.A. Crabtree's.' (*Ken Jeffrey*)

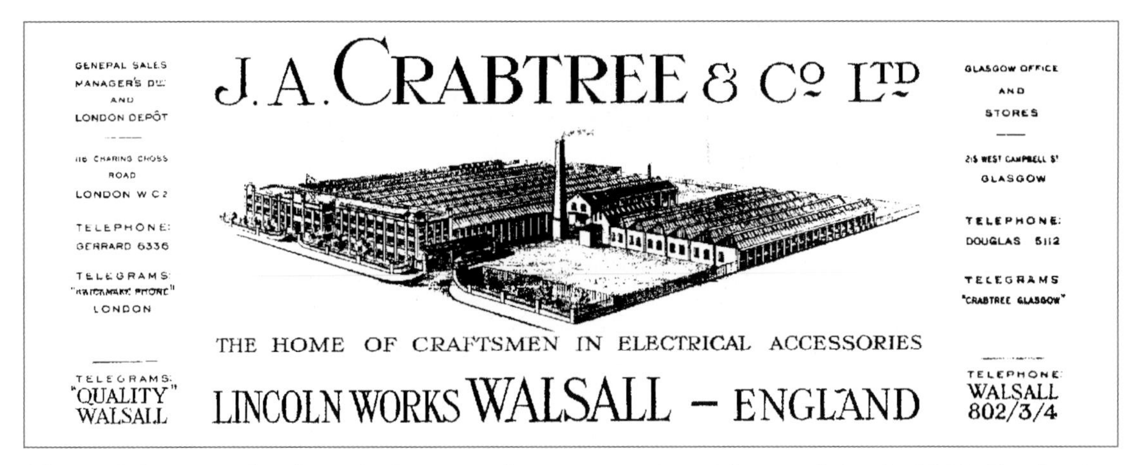

'This is Crabtree noteheading which was used to type a testimonial to my father in 1928. The drawing of the works shows how far it was developed at the beginning, because the site only opened in 1926, although the firm was established in Upper Rushall Street in 1919.' (*Ken Jeffrey*)

Dr Sethna remembers taking this picture of Reedswood Power Station one winter morning in the 1970s and that it did quite well in exhibitions for a time. Don Payne, President of Walsall Photographic Society, thinks this dramatic, frosty scene with billowing steam from the cooling towers epitomises the powerful capacity of this electricity generating station. When it was demolished a large amount of coal was also mined by open-cast methods, offsetting the cost of reinstatement as a retail park with domestic housing. (*Dr Sethna*)

The Walsall Power Station at Reedswood, cooling tower demolition, November 1984. Don Payne says, 'The larger part of the power station was post-Second World War and was opened officially by the Mayor, Cllr T.P. Riley on 30 September 1949. It was coal-burning and, eventually produced 200 megawatts at full power, although it was not complete at the official opening, only three of the planned six cooling towers having been built, for example. The original 1925 station, known as Birchills, remained as a small canal-side building receiving steam from the main station for power generation, when needed.' Walsall had been one of the first municipal authorities to generate electric power in 1890 and lost its power station only when coal-fired generating was no longer efficient. (*N. Canning*)

Mrs Hemminsley discovered this picture in her archives. 'It is Thomas Gameson and Son's Foundry, Lower Rushall Street in the 1960s. This was a well-established firm which advertised as early as 1905 as Malleable Ironfounders.' (*Mrs B. Hemminsley*)

'This is my husband, Stan Hemmingsley, at work at Gameson's Foundry, Lower Rushall Street, Walsall.' (*Mrs B. Hemminsley*)

'Arthur Farrington's photograph is an excellent atmospheric study of the wire machine workshop at Eyland and Sons, Lower Rushall Street, Walsall in the early 1900s.' (*John Griffiths*)

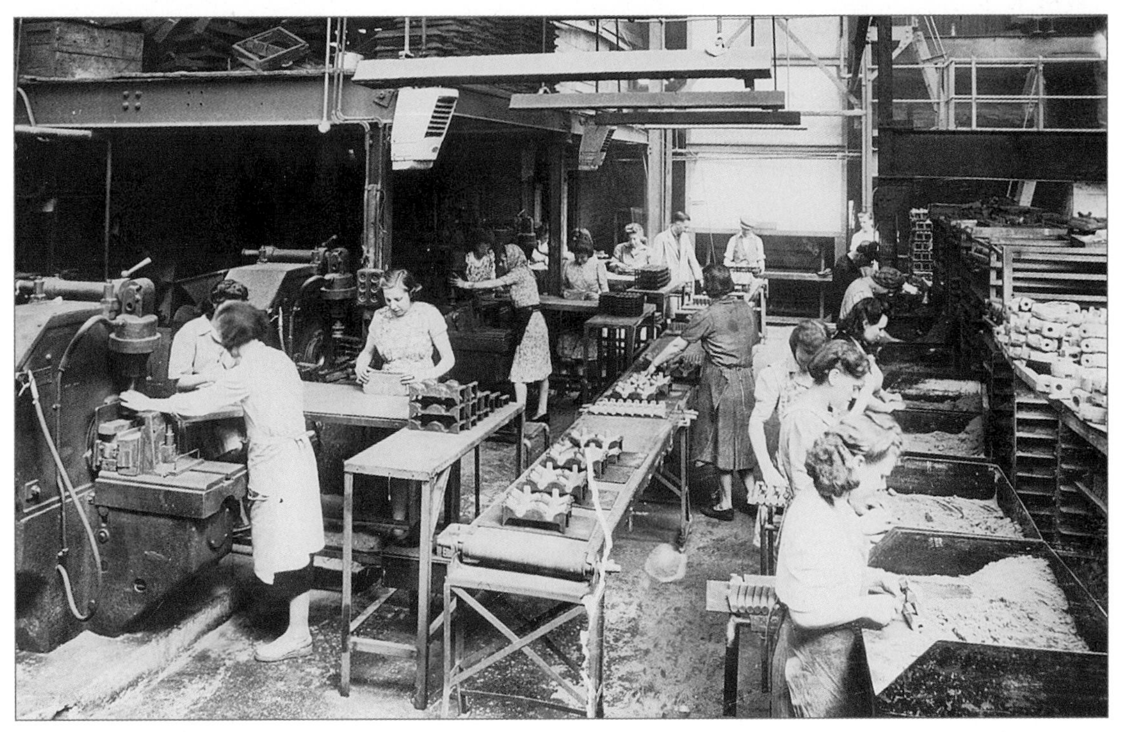

Mrs Barrie Benton says, 'this is my mother sorting aluminium at Frankels, Charles Street in the 1950s. She was called Amanda Parke and is second in from the right.' (*Mrs B. Benton*)

'This is Garrington's Albert Works, Darlaston, which had been established in new buildings in 1840 and closed down in 1993.' (*Garry Ashford-Smith*)

'Garringtons' Darlaston works added 6 acres by purchasing land from British Railways and installed the first new LASCO hammer/press in 1970, raising output to 135,000 tons.'
(*Garry Ashford-Smith*)

Peter Wright says, 'This is a range of components produced on Garrington's Lasco Hammer Presses. These were installed in the late 1960s or early 1970s and were extrusion presses with optional hammer blows. The picture includes hub ends for commercial vehicle axles, an axle shaft for JCB, a forging for the French oil industry (joint for drill pipes) and a shell for the MOD.'
(*Garry Ashford-Smith*)

This is a close-up of Massey 3-ton forge hammers at Garringtons. Eventually nos 56 and 57 were replaced by Beche hammers, and when they dug down a couple of feet for the foundations they reached water. Peter Wright identified the two men on the right as 'Major' Fletcher and Kenny ?. (*Garry Ashford-Smith*)

Peter Wright remembers that these Beche hammers were double-action hammers operated by compressed air to open and close the dies, and had been installed to produce radius arms for Land Rover. There is an example in the foreground, they were nicknamed 'shepherds' crooks'. These are now manufactured by Dudley Drop Forges. Left to right: B. Causer, D. Andrews, R. Holmes, W. Pringle, R. Fletcher, M. Tuckley. (*Garry Ashford-Smith*)

Peter Wright says, 'These 20cwt Massey hammers are being operated by Paddy Wilkins and A.N. Other.' (*Garry Ashford-Smith*)

'I took this picture of two Garringtons' presses being prepared for taking off site for scrapping. I was site manager in charge of closing the site of the former Albert Works.' (*Peter Wright*)

'A lot of my friends used to work in Gibbons' drawing office. We had many contracts with the Home Office for prisons and secure mental hospitals where we designed exterior locks, landing locks and cell locks, all with matching master and semi-master keys.' (*Albert Benbow*)

'I worked at Gibbons in this lock shop in Wolverhampton and joined my uncle, Harry Steadman. He died in about 1954 about four years after I joined. He went for a mass x-ray but didn't survive the operation on his lung.' (*Albert Benbow*)

'This is Gibbons' lock shop no. 2. My uncle, Harry Steadman, is fifth from the left, and next to him is Joey Whitehouse whose twin sons became university professors in the USA. There were three or four lock shops under one supervisor called Arthur Robbins snr. His son, Harry, was a charge-hand. Arthur was a chainsmoker and was known as "Gobber". He was known to stand for an hour watching the men.' (*Albert Benbow*)

This is the John Harper 'Albion Works' in Willenhall which was founded in 1790 by William Harper, producing such items as castings and spring latches, which by the end of the nineteenth century included lamp fittings, oil stoves, bicycles and tricycles. After the Second World War, the firm established itself in 1947 at the Albion Works in Clarkes Lane. By the 1950s, Harpers were facing keen competition over Electric Motor Stator castings and Tractor Axle castings. John Llewellyn, who left Harper's in 1969, remembers how the firm 'made malleable castings, sold on quality, and kept the motor industry at arm's-length'. (*Mrs P. Linney*)

Fred Parker is standing in front of huge castings manufactured at F.H. Lloyd's between 1960 and 1965. 'These were two 25-ton intermediate pressure cylinders for power generators for the electric power industry.' Left to right: Fred Parker (Supervisor), Ralph Hyde (Department Superintendent), Noel Briggs (Foreman), William Taylor (Works Manager), John Inett (Supervisor). Before it was closed down, F.H. Lloyd's gates used to boast that the firm was established in 1879 as steelfounders. (*Fred Parker*)

'This shows a packer dealing with ink tins at our firm, Manders in Wolverhampton.' (*Anthea Mander*)

'These are storage tanks at my family's firm Manders, Heath Town, Wolverhampton. I think you can just see St Peter's Church on the skyline.' (*Anthea Mander*)

'This is our Export Department at Manders, Heath Town. The names on the packing cases give plenty of clues to our worldwide trade.' (*Anthea Mander*)

Manders Old Inks Warehouse, Heath Town. (*Anthea Mander*)

'Standing around and looking at what I think must have been a new paint machine are C. Veldman, A.C. Fuller, G. Lilley and D. Momson.' (*Anthea Mander*)

Mushroom Green cottages, which were originally put up by chain-making families who were squatters on the edge of the commonland. Mrs Olwen Meller said, 'Step back in time as we visit the sleepy hamlet of Mushroom Green, where no two houses are alike and where the house numbers are anything but consecutive. On the left of the picture is Railway Cottage, a stone's throw from where John Wesley preached on his tour of the Black Country. "Musham", as it was then known, was famous for the chains made by the women in the small chain shops attached to their homes. In the middle of the twentieth century a favourite walk for locals was through Mushroom Green to view Jonah's garden – a sight to behold each summer with its wonderful display of flowers.'
(G. Warburton)

'This is a demonstration of chainmaking, Mushroom Green, in the 1970s. The community had grown up around the edge of the common, specialising in this industry. Demonstrations are organised regularly during the summer by the Black Country Living Museum.'
(D.F. Vodden)

'This shows one way in which women took part in ironworking, such as making edged tools or even chainmaking, probably around Cradley Heath. This may be a husband and wife making a pickaxe blade.'
(Geoff Warburton)

'This shows my aunt, Mrs Eleanor (Nell) Parnham, threading nuts at Nuts & Bolts which used to stand at the back of Slater Street School, Darlaston. The site is now a housing estate.' (*Bren Speed, from the Rotary Club, Darlaston Local History Society Collection*)

'I took this picture of the gates of the former Patent Shaft Steel Works, Leabrook Road, Wednesbury on 16 May 1990. The works, founded in 1834, had already been closed ten years and the site cleared apart from the gates in 1986.' (*Geoff Warburton*)

'I took these pictures at the Round Oak Steel Works during a visit by members of Walsall Chamber of Commerce in the 1950s.' (*Rex Stone*)

'Round Oak open pig beds, nineteenth century. At its peak in the 1850s the Black Country produced a quarter of British iron from 140 blast furnaces, and this continued well into the twentieth century. Molten iron flowed into a series of sand channels and, after cooling, were broken by hand into bars or pigs.' (*Geoff Warburton*)

Round Oak. (*Rex Stone*)

Rex Stone says, 'this is an interior which I took at the same occasion.' Ernie Bloomer remembers the steam crane 'which Wally Wadeley used to operate, and on the left is the smelting furnace and ingot moulds weighing 3 tons each which used to be taken to the soaking pits, rolling and cogging mill then to small furnaces to be formed into RSJs, T-bars and so on. My brother used to work at the Old Level across Level Street in the smaller mills.' (*Rex Stone*)

'Round Oak secured an order to supply special steel for extreme climatic conditions to be used in building the Labrador Bridge. Over 250 tons of our "Thirty-Oak" steel, capable of withstanding –40° centigrade were used.' (*Arthur Brummell*)

'When the Pensnett Rail branch line from The Wallows to Askew Bridge was closed, the last train was manned by D. Davies, M. Westbury, L. Smith, J. Lloyd and R. Hickinson, Wallows Traffic Supervisor.' (*Arthur Brummell*)

'This is how ingots for rolling were withdrawn from the oil-fired recuperative soaking pits at Round Oak in 1966.' (*Arthur Brummell*)

'This is a 37in Cogging Mill at Round Oak, capable of rolling ingots up to 5 tons in weight.' Don Scriven thinks that it closed down in 1982. (*Arthur Brummell*)

'Pickford's driver had difficulty getting on to the road in that bad winter with the beam for the University of Aston boiler house in 1952.' (*Ted Hickinbottom*)

'A 30-ton beam for the University of Aston leaving our Darlaston works in 1952.' (*Ted Hickinbottom*)

'I think the 30-ton beam is passing by the Darlaston Bullstake in this picture.' (*Ted Hickinbottom*)

'The 30-ton beam being carried in Darlaston. It is clear from this picture how desperately the Black Country infrastructure and particularly its road system needed radical overhaul. This wasn't achieved until the Black Country Development Corporation grasped the nettle.' (*Ted Hickinbottom*)

'Rubery Owen erecting the steel frame for Goodyear Tyres, Wolverhampton, on 14 November 1963. Very recently there has been talk of redundancies and even closure of the factory.' (*Ted Hickinbottom*)

'Rubery Owen won the contract for replacing the Horden Road Bridge in Wolverhampton.' (*Ted Hickinbottom*)

Putting the roadway in place. (*Ted Hickinbottom*)

Hordern Road bridge almost complete, 6 November 1968. It was to open six weeks later. (*Ted Hickinbottom*)

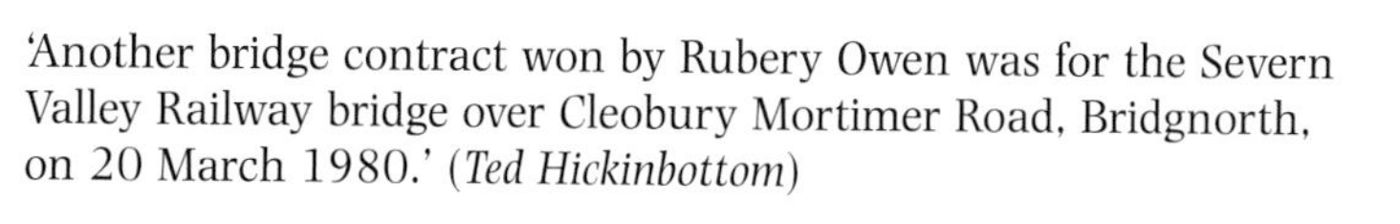

'Another bridge contract won by Rubery Owen was for the Severn Valley Railway bridge over Cleobury Mortimer Road, Bridgnorth, on 20 March 1980.' (*Ted Hickinbottom*)

'Billy Knowles was an expert electric welder at Rubery Owen who befriended me, and we used to socialise after work when I was sixteen to seventeen years old. He used to live in a back-to-back in Brades Village, Oldbury.' (*Ted Hickinbottom*)

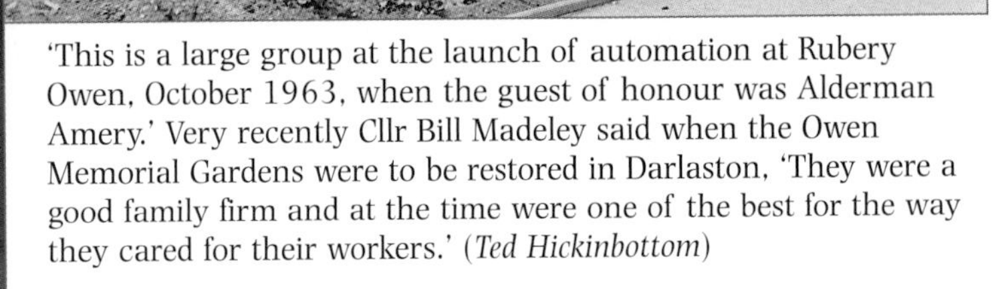

'This is a large group at the launch of automation at Rubery Owen, October 1963, when the guest of honour was Alderman Amery.' Very recently Cllr Bill Madeley said when the Owen Memorial Gardens were to be restored in Darlaston, 'They were a good family firm and at the time were one of the best for the way they cared for their workers.' (*Ted Hickinbottom*)

'Len Cashmore was a welding specialist at Rubery Owen. He came from West Bromwich and used to have a Triumph motorbike.' (*Ted Hickinbottom*)

'Cllr Jack Bedworth, who is the third left, I remember was also on the Board of the Wednesbury Building Society and the Committee of the Allotments Society. Fourth on the right is Jim Green. They are standing between huge plate girders at the Rubery Owen Darlaston Structural Division workshop, in about 1960.' (*Ted Hickinbottom*)

'These all-steel lifeboats were manufactured at Rubery Owen in the postwar years. This picture dates from March 1946.' (*Ted Hickinbottom*)

Brian Lowe says, 'I was involved in brass founding for many years. Our peak periods for sales were related to steam rallies, veteran car rallies and horse shows when we sold brass plaques and horse brasses galore. I took the following set of pictures at the Sandcast Foundry, Willenhall Casting recently to illustrate the whole process.'
(*Sandcast (B.H. Lowe) Foundry*)

Casting brass in upright boxes.
(*Sandcast (B.H. Lowe) Foundry*)

Moulding using an 'odd side'.
(*Sandcast (B.H. Lowe) Foundry*)

Bob Evans 'skimming the pot'.
(*Sandcast (B.H. Lowe) Foundry*)

The furnaces at Sandcast Foundry.
(*Sandcast (B.H. Lowe) Foundry*)

'A group of workers at Talbot Stead Co. in the 1950s. The firm was taken over by Tube Investments and the site in Green Lane has now been closed.'
(*Mrs L. Smithyman*)

'This is the welding shop and smithy at Wellman Smith Owen. My grandfather, Charlie Finch, is on the right. He joined the firm in 1920 and became the foreman of the welding shop. He died in October 1956 aged sixty-one.' (*Mrs G. Holmes*)

'This group of directors at Wellman Smith Owen, shows my grandfather, Charlie Finch, in the centre. The photograph may have been taken when he retired.' (*Mrs G. Holmes*)

'This was a WSO roller path made for a huge Khartoum-Omdurman bridge. I think the firm did a lot of contracts for bridges abroad.' (*Mrs G. Holmes*)

'This is a Wesley Smith Owen electric battery locomotive which I was told was built for Canadian mines. Apparently there was a big market over there for these.' (*Mrs G. Holmes*)

'I think these ingot handling machines were supplied to a large South Wales steelworks. They included ingot-stripping machines and charging machines all made by WSO.' (*Mrs G. Holmes*)

'These are "the girls" at Grandad's factory in Eldon Street. They were the machinists making leather clothing in about 1937. The firm's name was H. Bednall. Our aunt, Alice Bednall, is standing second from the right in the back row.' (*Nancy & Mary Sankey*)

'These are the cutters at H. Bednall leather clothing works in Eldon Street. Our grandfather, Harry Bednall, is at the back holding the door-frame. He started work in the early 1920s in Adam's Row as a saddler, having been apprenticed in the Haymarket, London.' (*Nancy & Mary Sankey*)

'This is a picture of Hawley's press room, where the men are busy cutting out linings.' (*Miss Lillian Hawley*)

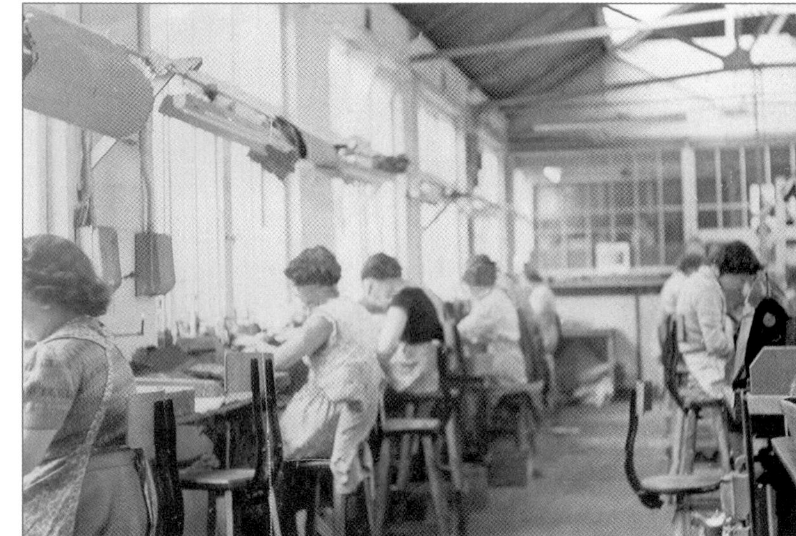

'This is Hawley's workshop where the women were able to work at their benches in well-lit surroundings.' (*Miss Lillian Hawley*)

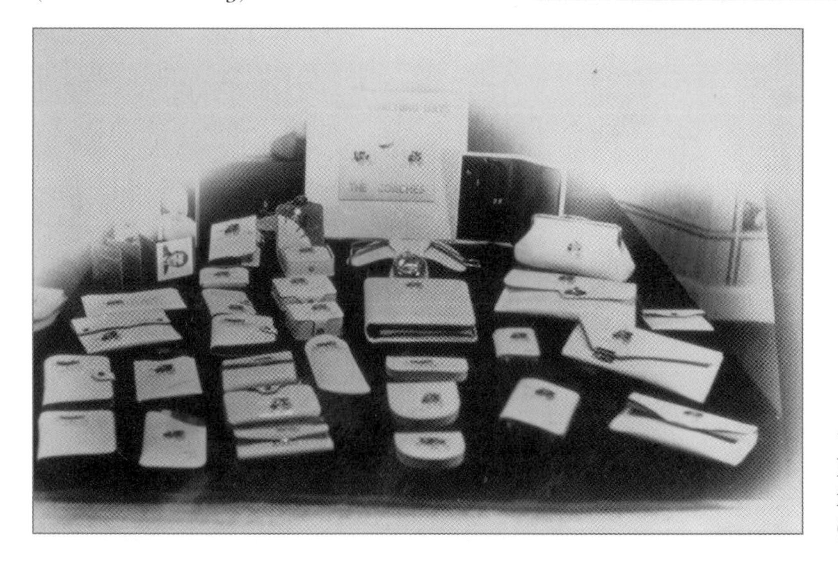

'This is a display of Hawley's leathergoods showing the wide range of fancy leathergoods we used to make.' (*Miss Lillian Hawley*)

'Harriett Collington is making riding crops in this picture taken at our firm of Hawley's.' (*Miss Lillian Hawley*)

After a long period of wrangling with the Borough Council, Asda dismantled their store in Darlaston in 2002 with a view to building a bigger and better one on a site which opened in November of that year. (*D.F. Vodden*)

'This is my mother's grocery shop situated at 74 Hollemeadow Avenue, Leamore, Walsall, decorated for the Queen's Coronation in 1953. There was a street party on the forecourt on Coronation Day.' (*Ken Baldwin*)

'My father Herbert Bird's butcher's shop, Oldbury. He is not in the picture, but butchering was in the family and Bert built up three businesses in the Smethwick and Oldbury area in the 1930s.' (*Mrs M. Wootton*)

'The Britannia Inn, 109 Kent Street, Lower Gornal was often known as "old Sal's". The building dates from 1780 and Sallie Perry ran it from 1942 until her death in 1991. It still had a rare taproom dating from 1900. Cow and Gate mild was the house ale until brewing ceased in 1964. The photograph was taken on 8 October 1991.' (*Geoff Warburton*)

'During the 1920s my father was a pianist for the silent pictures, and the piano-tuner for the various schools in the area, but when the "talkies" came in he was made redundant. He then decided to have this small shed erected in our garden at the corner of Franchise Street and Old Park Road. The children on the picture are his twin daughters, Marion on the trike and Dorothy beside her in 1928. Even in those days Father had trouble with stock being stolen, which decided him to move the business into the house.' (*Mrs M. Evans*)

'This was our second shop, 62 Old Park Road, King's Hill, which, after having a shop window put in the front room of our house, Father opened in the 1930s.' (*Mrs M. Evans*)

'Business progressed, and in about 1934 Father took over Sid Frost's Cycle Shop (8 Pinfold Street) on the Bull Stake. My parents retired from business in 1963. By this time we were a limited company, known as Len Mitchell Ltd, and together with a loyal staff we ran the business until 1982, when trade became impossible owing to road changes, and the closing down of the big factories around Darlaston. We had good days though – never to be forgotten.' (*Mrs M. Evans*)

'This was a newsagents and tobacco shop in High Bullen, Wednesbury. But I don't remember who the owners were.' (*E.D. Freeth*)

'This is Portland Street, Walsall, *c.* 1903, the place of business of W.H. Pennell, Coal, Coke and Breeze Merchants and General Haulier. David Pennell is standing by the cart, Peter Pennell is at the horse's head and father, W.H. Pennell, is standing by the window. Peter Pennell is my father. (*Mrs Kathleen Baldwin*)

Derek Pester, who has now retired to Chipping Campden, says, 'Grandfather Pester had this grocer's shop, built with its little cupola, in West Bromwich on the corner of Queen Street and High Street in 1912. It was sold in 1955 and, after being empty for a year, became a ladies' dress shop. It has since been demolished.' (*Derek Pester*)

Pester's shop photographed by Mr and Mrs Sidney Darby, professional photographers of New Street. (*Derek Pester*)

The Free Press 18th May 1900

YOU MAY BEAT KRUGER,
BUT YOU CAN'T BEAT
W. J. PESTER'S STORES
HIGH ST. AND BULL ST., WEST BROMWICH,
FOR HIGH-CLASS SUPPLIES OF
English & Foreign Fruits, Fresh & Cure
Fish, Game, Poultry, Rabbits, Vegetables, &c

PESTER'S—The Old-established Firm.
PESTER'S—For Quality all the year round.
PESTER'S—For Prompt Attention to Orders.
PESTER'S—For Private Families and Hotels.
PESTER'S—The Popular and Leading Stores.
PESTER'S—For Complete Satisfaction.

NO FAMINE OR WAR PRICES AT PESTER'S STORES
STEADY VALUE ALL THE YEAR ROUND.
The Road to PESTER'S is the Road to SATISFACTION

This extract from the *Free Press*, 1900, shows contemporary advertising humour. (*Derek Pester*)

Pester's, 214 High Street, West Bromwich. (*Derek Pester*)

'What a magnificent arrangement at the front of our grocer's in West Bromwich, and the family and staff were proud of it. We were the shop display winners in the 1920s.' (*Derek Pester*)

'My father and mother (wearing a frill), visited the *Athlone Castle* berthed at Southampton in 1936. They were interested in the transportation of fruit from abroad for their business, especially bananas.' (*Derek Pester*)

By direction of the Owners.

Particulars of Sale
of the
Exceedingly Valuable

FREEHOLD SHOP PROPERTY

Nos. 214 & 216, High Street
and Nos. 1/10, Queen Street
WEST BROMWICH

(Situate in the heart of one of the most prosperous Shopping Centres in the Midlands)

comprising :
TEN HIGH CLASS RETAIL SHOPS
and the OFFICE ACCOMMODATION on the Upper Floors.

Pester's shop sale notice for the auction at the Sandwell Hotel. (*Derek Pester*)

Lower Queen St., WEST BROMWICH

Telephone No.:
WESt Bromwich 0084

M.. 193
DR. TO

W. J. Pester & Sons

(Partners: F. PESTER, C. H. PESTER)

FISH SHOP

Weekly Payments Prompt

No Deductions allowed

No receipt is valid unless on Printed Form

Billhead, W.J. Pester & Sons, 1930s. (*Derek Pester*)

John Griffiths describes the Round of Beef, Colley Gate, Cradley, as 'a one-family watering hole for 138 years'. 'There can be few, if any readers alive today who remember the Round of Beef at Colley Gate as it was in this photograph from around the 1890s. At that time the landlord was Thomas Cox, his name clearly visible on the sign, who reigned as landlord from 1890 to 1896. Could that be him standing in the doorway or maybe one of the others in the picture? On a recent visit to the Round the present landlord, Mervyn Jarvis, showed me a framed history of the pub complete with all the landlords. Incredibly the licence stayed in the Cox family for 138 years, from Edwin Cox in 1844 through to Norman Cox in 1982.' (*John Griffiths*)

'Stantons' wet fish shop, Wednesbury, which I photographed on 25 March 1992. This was the last open-fronted slab in the UK and closed in the autumn of 1992.' (*Geoff Warburton*)

'I took this picture of Merry Hill in March 1989 to show the birth of the new complex. We went round as a group of "Green Badge" aspirants and I went back later to capture the "naissance" of the development. Sadly the former monorail track which comes into the picture from the left has all but gone, but the canal here has been cleared out and re-routed to create more land for Merry Hill which still has to be utilised.' (*Geoff Warburton*)

3

Transport

'This is a picture of my grandfather, Joseph Meller, driving a coach outside the hospital, Pleck Road, in the early 1900s. He was the coachman for the managing director of Walker Brothers of Pleck and lived to the age of ninety-one, dying in 1969. Walker Brothers used to manufacture galvanised, corrugated and flat sheets for all purposes including iron buildings, Dutch barns, buckets, dustbins, wire netting and iron fencing.' (*Roy Meller*)

'This is the horse-drawn delivery cart of Attkins and Son, grocers and wine and spirit merchants, of 5 Park Street, who were the family grocer of the Farringtons. The photo was taken by Arthur or Frank Farrington.' (*John Griffiths*)

'I took this picture of the Star 18/5 Comet with Mr Lister driving. His uncle was managing director of the local firm which built only three of this model.' (*Geoff Warburton*)

'This motorcycle rally caught my eye at the Black Country Living Museum on 17 September 1994. There are Sunbeams, an AJS 350cc OHV (1927), an AJS 350cc GS with Semi TT handlebars, and a 1928 V-twin 8-hp model. Steve Mills of Sutton Coldfield had restored the K1, the last of the flat twins.' (*Geoff Warburton*)

'I was at the unveiling of the AJS sculpture, which was carved by Robert Bowers, 31 August 1996. He was a local boy who attended Kates Hill School, 1975–86, when I was headmaster there. The memorial is carved from a 10 ton block of Grifton Wood limestone from the Francis N. Lowe Quarry, Derbyshire. The work took seven months and was taken to the site in three sections.' (*Geoff Warburton*)

'These Westfield sports cars were manufactured from the early 1980s by Chris Smith of Lotus at Armytage. In 1985 manufacture moved to Pensnett in order to expand. They were probably the largest kit car manufacturers in Europe. They were the first British kit-car manufacturer to receive low-volume type approval, and the cars do not need 'Q' plates. I think this is a true success story.' (*Geoff Warburton*)

In 1967 Everton's opened a new ultra-modern main depot garage in Long Lane, Blackheath. They were also the first to provide self-service petrol pumps in the Midlands. This was a matter for regret later. As Robert Everton says, 'When you act as guinea pigs like that, you bear the cost of development and competitors eventually benefit.' (*R. Everton*)

'We did body work for commercial vehicles such as this Oldbury Transport truck.' (*R. Everton*)

S. Priest's Guy lorry. (*R. Everton*)

'Horace Kendrick of Walsall's truck when newly painted. We didn't do this job, but include it because of the Walsall connection.' (*R. Everton*)

BP tanker after painting by Evertons. (*R. Everton*)

Robert Everton remembers how this eight-wheeler truck hit the Shenstone pub at the bottom of Mucklow Hill one Friday afternoon in the 1960s. The pub was rebuilt after the accident, but soon demolished to make way for a traffic island. Everton's of Blackheath recovered the lorry at a quiet time on Sunday morning. (*R. Everton*)

Roy Meller says, 'I think this two-car collision took place in the late 1930s on Walsall's Broadway West. It seems to be at the junction with Alexandra Road. This type of incident is less likely now because there is a 30 mph speed limit, road surfaces are better, brakes and tyres are of a better design and maintained better because of the annual MOT test.' (*Roy Meller*)

Jim Shelley is proud of his 1927/32 12–50 Lambourne-bodied ducksback Alvis. 'It is completely rebuilt and restored to 1927 specification. The car, which was to beat the Bugattis and all comers in the 200-mile race, arrived in 1923. My first car was an Alvis 12–50 Beetleback.' (*Jim Shelley*)

Len Onslow with Super Onslow Special road bike. These were produced in both air- and water-cooled versions. One of Len's greatest achievements was to win the Brighton speed trials in 1930 on a 172cc machine of his own design at 88mph. He was awarded the MBE for services to motor cycling and featured in *This Is Your Life* in 1999, and soon afterwards reached 100 years old. (*Jim Shelley*)

'I took this picture of a Dudley trolley bus at the entrance to the transport shed at the Black Country Living Museum in March 1990. It is a Sunbeam W built in 1946 with a Park Royal utility body.' (*Geoff Warburton*)

'My father, Bert Newman, was a signwriter with Walsall Corporation. In 1951 he decorated this Walsall bus and another to mark the Festival of Britain. The lighting was done by George Mountford, the Corporation electrical engineer.' (*Alan Newman*)

'I took this picture at the Black Country Museum, in March 1990, of this former Walsall trolley bus. It used to run on the Walsall–Bloxwich route. The service opened on 1 October 1933 and the last run was completed on 3 October 1970.' (*Geoff Warburton*)

A Walsall trolley bus near The Eagle on the Walsall–Bloxwich route. (*R. Everton*)

Overhead cable maintenance in Walsall. (*R. Everton*)

Trolley buses on the Bloxwich route on The Bridge, 1950. (*R.A. Brevitt*)

'I remember how Dartmouth Garage used to be situated in Church Vale just past the junction with Hallam Street. This dates from 1935. Not far away, behind the site of the present hospital, there used to be nailers' cottages which were three steps down from the street and the earth floors used to be covered with greenery.' (*Derek Pester*)

'I took this canal bridge at Bumblehole, Netherton, while I was on a photography City and Guilds course at Halesowen College because it caught my eye and reminds me of the Black Country's industrial success.' (*Brian Simmonds*)

'I took this picture of the newly rebuilt Neville Garratt Bridge on a canal walk on 17 October 1999 on the Stourbridge Arm which runs for 1½ miles into the heart of Stourbridge. It presaged the arrival of Bradley's Ironworks in 1850 on the canal banks here. The bonded warehouse in the background had returned almost to its original spot from the Black Country Living Museum.' (*Geoff Warburton*)

'The following week, on 24 October 1999, I took this picture looking north from Neville Garratt Bridge showing the last boats from the previous week's rally. It shows interesting canal brickwork and slopes, blended to fit in, and yet is functional for passers-by and modern tourists. The distant towpath has strong evidence of old ironworks and canal-side cranes, looking to the main Stourbridge Canal from Stewponey south and west to Dudley and the Black Country Living Museum in the north. (*Geoff Warburton*)

'The canal from Neville Garratt Bridge towards Wolverhampton. The bridge was originally inscribed "John Bradley & Co., Stourbridge, 1838" and was conserved at the Black Country Living Museum before re-erecting, 1999.' (*Geoff Warburton*)

'This was a demonstration of making fenders at the Bonded Warehouse, 17 October 1999. These cost £50 large, £30 small. Not too much considering the time and skill entailed.' (*Geoff Warburton*)

Fred Parker and his brother recognised these old petrol pumps in Park Lane, Fallings Heath standing on the site of T.L. Harvey's original garage. The firm has now moved its main site to the Heath Road area where they dismantle vehicles. (*D.F. Vodden*)

Bob Bibby described this scene in his *Grey Paes & Bacon*: 'Telford's route runs spectacularly through a steep-sided forty-foot deep cutting. . . . Above us to our left was the main West Coast railway line and beyond that we could see the pale concrete stilts that carry the M5 motorway through the Black Country. . . . Some spectacular bridges are evident here – the motorway stilting itself, the Telford Aqueduct that takes a short stretch from the old Brindley line over the newer line, the impressive Galton Bridge with its one hundred and fifty-feet cast iron span, and the Steward Aqueduct where the old line crosses the new line parallel to the motorway.' (*Geoff Warburton*)

J. Hubble says, 'This was located in Tipton (Five Ways) Goods Depot and was ex-GWR. I had that depot as a canal depot and used it for testing and loading chains. There were rollers on the canal side to take chain to be taken out of the boats to the test house. I never operated the depot as a chain depot and I think I let out the test house. I never operated the bridge as a lifting bridge and it was simply used as a cartway for its last few years there. I was Goods Agent, Dudley, 1959–60.'

The lifting bridge is being dismantled for it to be moved to the Staffordshire County Museum. The bridge had already been damaged by vandals. With Government approval (as it is a listed ancient monument), it was transferred to the Black Country Living Museum, Dudley. (*BCLM Collection*)

The canal lifting bridge from Tipton Goods Depot as it is at the Black Country Living Museum. (*D.F. Vodden*)

'The first new canal section for generations was dug at Brierley Hill to divert it away from proposed road development. This had just been drained to deal with a leak, 27 March 1998.' (*Geoff Warburton*)

'This shows me with other railway workers at the Ryecroft Shed. I joined the railway at sixteen and a half in 1949. I soon transferred from being a 'knocker-upper', which meant waking up drivers on my bike in Walsall and Bescot to cleaner. I was about to become a fireman when I left to join the army.' (*Ron Davies*)

'This picture shows my grandfather, George Cartwright, who was born in about 1899, in a gang of other platelayers. I think it was taken in West Bromwich where he lived all his life.' (*Mrs A. Souster*)

'Charles Instance was born in 1864 and worked as a "caster" on the railway.' (*Mrs G. Holmes*)

'This is the site of the old Dudley station site, 2 June 1995, looking north along the railway (LMS and GWR) from Castle Hill Bridge to the left of the Tipton Road.' (*Geoff Warburton*)

'I come from Wednesbury and this is the tram terminal outside the White Horse. On the left is the old Lloyds Bank, the firm I worked for, but not this branch.' (*Mrs Barbara Wakelin*)

'This is the Metro tramway terminus under construction on 21 July 1997 looking from Bilston Street Northwest at the junction of Garrick Street and Bilston Street, Wolverhampton.' (*Geoff Warburton*)

'I took this picture of a Metro practice-run in May 1999 before the official opening in June.' (*Geoff Warburton*)

'A Metro leaving Wolverhampton, 23 September 1999, over the road bridge and underpass to all directions. The new police station is in red brick to the left of the bridge. This is a taste of the new millennium!' (*Geoff Warburton*)

Geoff Warburton says, 'I took this picture of the monorail at Merry Hill on 4 December 1992. It is now gone.' Ned Williams regrets its passing. 'The public service transport system for Merry Hill has not yet been solved. The offices on the Waterfront could do with better communications. When it was running, you got a great view from up on the monorail train.' (*Geoff Warburton*)

'I took this view of the monorail passing Netherton church, centre background, on 5 February 1993. It was an example of "ancient and modern".' (*Geoff Warburton*)

'Merry Hill monorail crossing Level Street, 14 May 1991.' (*Geoff Warburton*)

4

Local Government & Royal Visits

Former Police Sergeant Ted Knight recalls, 'The Willenhall Police on parade outside the station before going on duty on Coronation Day, 1953. Front row, left to right: Sergeant Stan Fullerton, PC Ted Knight, PC Don Wilkes, Superintendant Green, Inspector Cogbill, Sergeant Ted Lacey. Back row: PCs Tom Izon, Arthur Allen, Norman Tonkinson, Harry Whittaker. All are wearing caps because the Staffordshire County Police did not wear helmets.' (*Ted Knight*)

'This was the day the Queen arrived at Crabtree's, Lincoln Works, Beacon Street, entrance in Walsall, on 24 May 1962.' (*Ken Jeffrey*)

The official programme stated, 'HM the Queen welcomed to Crabtree's in 1962.' Sadly, the Lincoln Works has now gone. Alan Preston says, 'The Crabtree motto, "That which is built soundly endures well," was right for the Works, because it lasted a good eighty years, which is longer than many more modern ones last, nowadays.' (*Ken Jeffrey*)

'J. Crabtree introducing Lieutenant Colonel Day, Messrs C. Etherington, A. Harper and T. Wintle to HM The Queen.' (*Ken Jeffrey*)

Alex the hairdresser says, 'I can remember the day of the Queen's visit. This shows the royal car leaving Crabtree's in Beacon Street, Walsall. On the day, the filming was done from my flat roof.' (*Ken Jeffrey*)

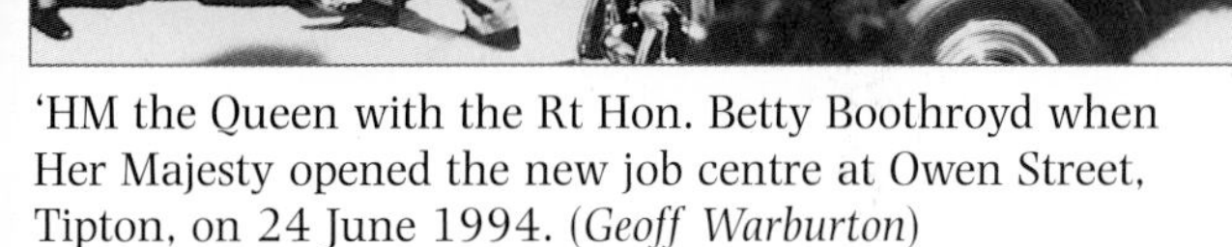

'HM the Queen with the Rt Hon. Betty Boothroyd when Her Majesty opened the new job centre at Owen Street, Tipton, on 24 June 1994. (*Geoff Warburton*)

'This shows HM the Queen being greeted by the Mayor of Walsall, Cllr Keith Sears, when she visited Walsall on 24 June 1994 to open the new Probation Training Centre in Tasker Street.' (*D.F. Vodden*)

'This was the occasion when Princess Diana, as patron, visited Relate offices, Lower Hall Lane, Walsall, in 1991. She arrived quite late having paused *en route* to comfort close friends over their child.' (*D.F. Vodden*)

'The Princess Diana statue in black granite was being displayed at the new Walsall bus station in 2001. There is on-going discussion of a final resting-place for it, although it was given to the town by the sculptor, monumental mason Mr Andrew Walsh.' (*D.F. Vodden*)

Stan Hill, Chairman of Brierley Hill Urban District Council, leading the parade to the Civic Service at St Michael's parish church, Brierley Hill, 19 June 1955. 'Having first been elected a councillor in 1952 at the age of twenty-three, it was reported that I was the youngest civic head in the country when I was twenty-six! At a Royal Reception in Stafford, I responded to Prince Philip's enquiry by translating the council's motto, "Sine Labore Nihil Floret".' (*Stan Hill*)

Stephen Parkes says, 'My mother, Mayor Vi Parkes, in civic procession to St Matthew's church, Walsall, 1980. She is followed by Deputy Mayor Phil Wood, Town Clerk Mr Galloway and Father Simister. All the buildings in the background in Digbeth have changed hands and, in the case of Ratners, formerly Craddocks, have been totally replaced.' (*D.F. Vodden*)

THE RT. HON.
JOHN STONEHOUSE
YOUR CANDIDATE

The Rt. Hon. John Stonehouse was elected Member of Parliament for Wednesbury in the famous by-election in 1957. As a back bencher he was very active on a wide range of issues and was appointed a Parliamentary Member of the Council of Europe from 1962 to 1964.

In 1964 he became Parliamentary Secretary in the Ministry of Aviation and was responsible for helping Britain's aircraft export drive in many countries. Later he was made Parliamentary Under Secretary of State for the Colonies and led Britain's delegation to the Independence celebrations in Botswana and Lesotho.

John Stonehouse became Privy Councillor in 1968 when he was Minister of State, Technology and Minister of Aviation. In this position he led for Britain in many international negotiations on Concorde and other projects. He was the leader of the British delegation to the Soviet aircraft industry and toured most aircraft plants in the United States, helping to promote British component sales. He helped Rolls Royce to achieve the sale of a British aero engine for the American Lockheed Tri Star—worth hundreds of millions of pounds in exports.

He was promoted to Postmaster General in 1968 and guided the massive Post Office Act through Parliament to set up the Post Office Corporation.

John Stonehouse is an economist (graduating with B.Sc.(Econ.) from London University) and is a specialist in promoting British exports. He is married with three children.

During his 18 years as Member of Parliament for Wednesbury and Walsall, John Stonehouse has always been available to constituents for help and advice. Every few weeks he has held an Advice Service. He will continue to hold these for constituents in Walsall North.

VOTE LABOUR on October 10th
7 a.m. to 10 p.m.

YOU CAN HELP LABOUR IN
THIS CAMPAIGN BY CONTACTING ANY
COMMITTEE ROOM OR
CENTRAL COMMITTEE ROOMS
Tel: BLOXWICH 401305

JOHN STONEHOUSE SPEAKS
AT LABOUR'S ELECTION
MEETINGS ON :

TUESDAY, 8th OCTOBER
7-30 p.m.
POOL HAYES SCHOOL,
CASTLE DRIVE

8-0 p.m.
BEACON ROAD SCHOOL,
NEW INVENTION

WEDNESDAY, 9th OCTOBER
7-30 p.m.
FOREST SCHOOL,
HAWBUSH ROAD

8-0 p.m.
GREEN ROCK SCHOOL,
BLAKENHALL

FOR A BETTER
BRITAIN

'It's important to remember the good work John Stonehouse did for people in the area before he got into trouble (see page 157). This is an election address for Walsall North, 1974.' (*Ian Payne*)

'John Stonehouse (left) as Aviation Minister in 1965 with his PPS, Smethwick MP Andrew Faulds (second on the right). (*Ian Payne*)

When Walsall were promoted to the Second Division they were given a Civic Banquet in 1961. The Chairman was Ernest Thomas and the Mayor was Mrs A.M.M. Taylor.' (*Tony Matthews*)

COUNTY BOROUGH OF WALSALL

CIVIC BANQUET

to

WALSALL FOOTBALL CLUB

on their Promotion to the Second Division

of the Football League

1960-1961

•

TOWN HALL, WALSALL

FRIDAY, 21st JULY, 1961

'My mother gave me this picture of Wolverhampton Hospital staff in 1923 when she was working there as a nurse. I'm afraid I don't know any of the names.' (*Mrs Pat Linney*)

This is a picture of Willenhall Urban District Council when my father was chairman.' (*Mrs Pat Linney*)

'This shows my father as Chairman leading the Willenhall Urban District Council church parade.' (*Mrs Pat Linney*)

The gate to the former Fred Evans Old People's Home, Walsall. The home has now been demolished and the site sold to Bryant Homes for development as sixty-six apartments. (*D.F. Vodden*)

The former Fred Evans Home boarded up in 2001 ready for sale and demolition. The Local Authority had made the decision to close, partly because a European directive required all homes for old people to be upgraded with en-suite facilities within twelve years. The cost was expected to be excessive. Only the former Wheway family home, 'The Shubbery' is to be retained and converted into a further four apartments. (*D.F. Vodden*)

5

War & Celebrations

'This rare picture is of the Walsall Volunteers' return from the Boer War on 21 May 1902. Arthur Farrington took at least three sequence shots of this occasion, no mean feat with a quarter-plate camera. I believe the photographs were taken from the middle or top floor of Ennals and Co.' (*John Griffiths*)

'This is a platoon of Grenadier Guards in the First World War. William Frederick Harrison is second from the right in the front row. He came out of the war without a scratch and applied to join the Walsall Borough Police. However, he contracted TB and died at the Pelsall Sanatorium at the age of twenty-four.' (*Terry Harrison*)

'This shows my uncle, Bert Williams, who lived in Tividale, serving in the Church Army with an army chaplain during the First World War.' (*Mrs Garrington, née Williams*)

This 'Poem of the South Staffs' was discovered by the late Freda Allen who said, 'It is a poignant reminder of the First World War and the feelings of a local lad who, with other working men, especially coal miners, went to do their bit for King and Country.' (*the late Freda Allen*)

Poem of the South Staffs

Here's to the Faithful Staffords,
The boys who are so dear,
Who answered their country's call
Without a doubt or fear.
At Backworth some are staying
With rifles, bayonets, and guns,
To make their training most perfect
Before they meet the Huns.

Hundreds of them were miners,
And they are sadly missed,
Who are to-day in the trenches
Instead of being in the pits.
They think of homes from whence they came,
And wonder if they are the same.

Results may be poor and faulty,
Failures we often are;
Remember it isn't the brightest
That makes the lovliest star.
It may not be worth your trouble
To try your luck with the rest,
But remember the pride of the country
Are trying to do their best.

Think of the bright romantic youth
Who's gone to fight for perfect peace;
To Britons true it has no charms,
And he who would to bloodshed yield
I would place him first upon the field,
As I think of bitter tears
Of those who are advanced in years,
It makes one study and declare
That this wide world is full of care.

Sometimes their lips in joy declare
That they are all quite happy there;
Yet they would rather peaceful dwell
Instead of chaos, shot, and shell
They hoist their flags and float them high,
With dauntless brow and piercing eye;
The only music is the drum
Which hails the triumph yet to come.

Here's to our gallant heroes,
Who keep the flag on high,
Sometimes they think of homeland's shore,
And hear a cry unheard before –
The cry which calls them to defend
Great Britain's name – a faithful friend.

'I took this picture of Lye War Memorial on 15 January 1990. It was set up on 23 October 1926, designed by Stanley Harley.' (*Geoff Warburton*)

'I think this was a Remembrance Day parade at Darlaston Football Club ground after the First World War.' (*Mrs G. Holmes*)

'The Earl of Dudley talking to my father, John T. Harrison, when he was in Civil Defence in about 1941.' (*Terry Harrison*)

J. A. CRABTREE & CO. LTD., LINCOLN WORKS, WALSALL

WORKS PASS

Reference : Date 17th Nov. 1941.

Name : Kenneth M. Jeffrey,

Address : 92, Beacon Street, Walsall.

National Registration Number : OOOM | 114 | 3

Department : Tool Room Check Number : 41

Holder's Signature : Kenneth M. Jeffrey.

This pass is the property of J. A. Crabtree & Co. Ltd. and must be given up on request. It is not transferable and must be available on entering and leaving the Works.

Anyone finding this pass is asked to post it to J. A. Crabtree & Co. Ltd., Lincoln Works, Walsall, Staffs. Postage will be refunded.

'This is my wartime works pass from J.A. Crabtree's which was issued in 1941. I don't think I was ever asked to show it!' (*Ken Jeffrey*)

'This is my identity card from the Second World War. During the war I served in the ARP.' (*Miss Lillian Hawley*)

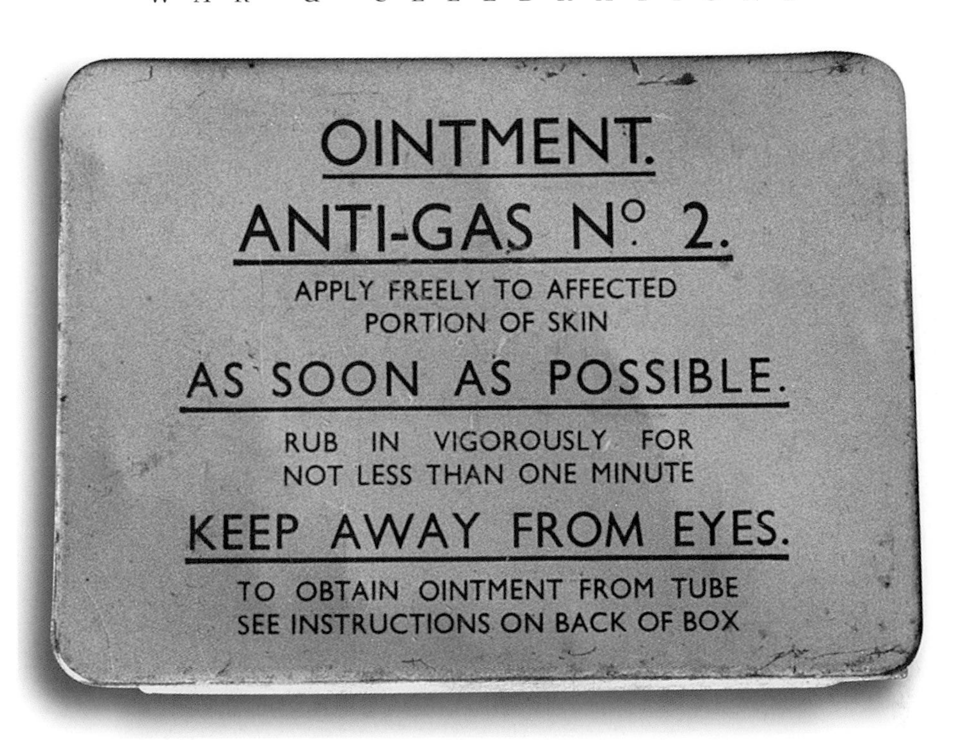

'This is a tin of Anti-Gas ointment which was issued in case mustard gas was used by the Germans in an air raid.' (*Miss Lillian Hawley*)

'The tubes of Anti-Gas ointment were never used because the Germans didn't use mustard gas as first feared.' (*Miss Lillian Hawley*)

Above left: 'We had this ration book cover with Tate & Lyle's "Mr Cube" on it.' (*Miss Lillian Hawley*)

Above right: 'This shrapnel was from a bomb which landed on the Broadway, Walsall, and damaged some houses opposite what is now the University of Wolverhampton sports field.' (*Miss Lillian Hawley*)

'My sister, Kathleen Arlene Harrison, volunteered to serve in the Women's Land Army in the Second World War and went to work in Cambridgeshire.' (*Terry Harrison*)

'Kathleen Harrison in the Land Army in Cambridgeshire during the Second World War with carthorse Charlie.' (*Terry Harrison*)

'This is my sister Kathleen on a Fordson tractor at a farm in Abingdon Piggotts, owned by farmer Thomas Russell Barnes. She enjoyed working there in the Land Army so much that she married the farmer.' (*Terry Harrison*)

'This is the local South Staffordshire Home Guard in 1944 and was probably taken at GKN, Sutton Road, Darlaston, where they often met. My father, Sergeant Leslie Speed, is in the front row, fourth from the right.' (*Bren Speed*)

'I took these pictures of a War Weapons Week parade in the middle of Walsall.' (*Rex Stone*)

'This is a picture I took of GIs playing baseball during the latter part of the Second World War at the Cricket Club in Gorway, Walsall.' (*Rex Stone*)

'This is a rocket projector made for the War Office during the Second World War by Rubery Owen, 23 May 1944.' (*E. Hickinbottom*)

'I took this picture of the VE Day parade on The Bridge, Walsall, on 8 May 1945. Note the static water tank which was there for the Fire Brigade to use. (*Rex Stone*)

'I was only a babe in arms at this VE Day street party in Darlaston. My mother is holding me up, and standing next to us is my aunt.' (*Bren Speed*)

Alan Newman says, 'This shows 5th Battalion South Staffs TA in 1958 marching 100 miles in four days to Nijmegen. Left to right: George Smith, Sergeant Jones, RSM Price, Evans, me (Alan Newman), Lunn, Morrall, Ted Wilkes, Captain Jones, Corporal Bill Glover, Lieutenant Colonel James, Captain Squires. ' (*Alan Newman*)

'This is a Coronation Day party, June 1953, at the rear of 6 the Flatts, Darlaston, the home of Mr and Mrs Plant and their twins Ronald and Sheila (in the front of picture). Back row, left to right: Florence Parker, Florrie Plant, Cyril Plant, Dennis Parker, Wilf Parker, June Plant, Margaret Tonks. Middle row: Derek Hammond, Graham Woodward, Vera Fletcher, Betty Titley, John Fletcher, George Thomas and John Robinson.' (*Fred Parker*)

'This is the last prefab at Sargent's Hill, Walsall, which belonged to Sandwell MBC. Mrs Betty Barratt alerted me to the proposal to remove it. It has now been demolished and the whole site sold for redevelopment for private domestic housing, which is being constructed very quickly and will soon be occupied.' (*D.F. Vodden*)

6

Social Life, Sports & Leisure

'This is one of myself and my eldest daughter with monkey at the Bloxwich Carnival in 1958.' (*Mrs B. Hemminsley, née Griffiths*)

'Harry Watts and his band were playing in the Arboretum Bandstand, Walsall. Stan Tinkler was on the piano, Les Bailey, tenor and Wilf Hawley, alto.' (*Jim Shelley*)

'Harry Watts' band with vocalist Ida Taylor. Vocals, I remember, were later supplied by Frances Dee.' (*Jim Shelley*)

'This is a picture of my late wife, Hazel, on the Arboretum lake, Walsall, during the severe winter of 1962 when it froze over completely.' (*Roy Taylor*)

'I was at a dinner in December 1961 at the Thornecroft Hotel with my friends, Alan Graham, Nicolette ?, Michael Elwell, Vicki Beattie, Victoria Oakley and Michael Ceble.' (*Anthea Mander*)

'This is an old picture of Maypole dancers outside St John's, Sams Lane, West Bromwich, in 1911.' (*Miss R. Trow*)

'Maypole dancers, 1914'. (*Miss R. Trow*)

'The date on the back of this picture is 1925, and Father is standing on the left (I can't name the other gentleman). This was when father worked as pianist at the Picturedrome, and sometimes at the Olympia down Darlaston Green.' (*Mary & Ted Evans*)

'This is the former Davilo Cinema, Old Swinford Road, Stourbridge, which later became the Odeon, seen here on 13 July 1995.' (*Geoff Warburton*)

'The Old Central Theatre was opened on 16 May 1929 by Ernest Stevens with Lori's *Crucifixion* as the first performance. It was adapted for "talkies" in April 1930 and became the Odeon in 1938. Designed by Webb and Grey, it had 1,500 seats and a £4,000 Compton organ. It is seen here on 6 April 1995.' (*Geoff Warburton*)

'Oakeswell Hall, Walsall Road, Wednesbury, was the family home of Dr Garman. His daughter Kathleen became the second wife of Sir Jacob Epstein, and on Sir Jacob's death she formed an art collection based on some of his own works and items collected by herself and her friend Sally Ryan. Lady Epstein stipulated in her will that the Garman-Ryan Collection should be housed in the Midlands. Unfortunately Oakeswell Hall, the former family home, first mentioned in 1421 and, after the Garmans, bought in 1952 by the Parton family, was subsequently the subject of a compulsory purchase order in 1956 to use it as a hostel for local Technical College students. There were plans to demolish and rebuild it, as it had been in a poor state of repair; it was demolished in 1982. The art collection went to Walsall Art Gallery and is now housed in the New Art Gallery, Walsall.' (*Mrs T. Parton*)

Oakeswell Hall interior. (*Mrs T. Parton*)

Jo Digger says, 'New Art Gallery, Walsall, is both a world-class art gallery and a work of important contemporary architecture, built in the heart of Walsall. People from all over the world visit the gallery with nearly half a million visitors in the first two years, contributing to the economic regeneration of the region. It is a fantastic facility for everyone, children and adults alike, with education at the heart of its philosophy. It is a place that breaks down many of the conventional views of who and what art galleries are for.' (*D.F. Vodden*)

Peter Wright remembers T. Chapman of Sandy Lane who was Chairman of the Evergreen Room 1961–72, seen here with Lord Brookes and Lord Brookes' portrait, which hung in the Evergreen Room, Darlaston. See page 138 for more about the Evergreen Room. (*Garry Ashford-Smith*)

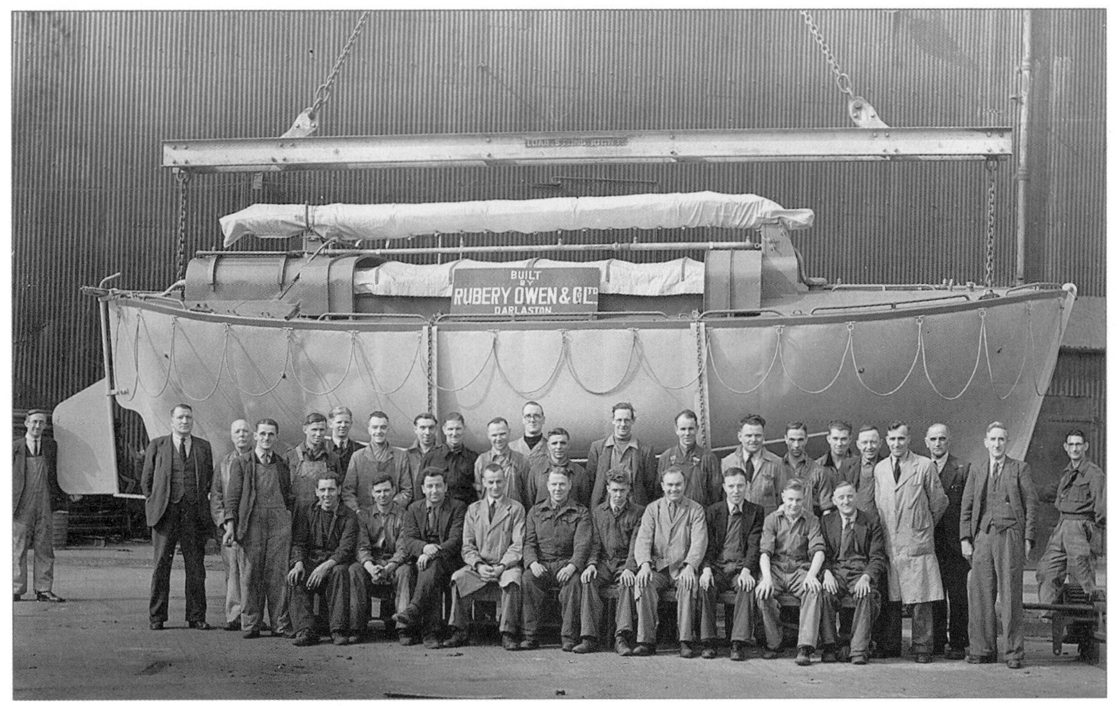

'This is a picture of the Works team with a lifeboat in 1946. I don't remember all the names but the photograph includes the following: Jack Walters, Joe Gee, Ted Roberts, Alf Bate, Ray Wilkinson, Jack Hedge and Henry Corns.' (*E. Hickinbottom*)

Miss Lillian Hawley, now eighty-six, says, 'All the firm's employees were invited to my twenty-first birthday party in 1938.' (*Miss Lillian Hawley*)

'Peter Yates, who took over the family firm, looks on while I receive bouquets on my retirement in 1979.' (*Miss Lillian Hawley*)

'This was an outing to Blackpool in 1955 organised by customers of the Spring Cottage, Elmore Green, Bloxwich.' (*Peter O'Brien*)

'This is an eighteenth-century pub known originally as the Throttler because it was kept by Betty Kemp, the local executioner. It stands over the Gorsty Canal Tunnel and re-opened in March, 1992 as the Lighthouse, with a nautical theme interior. I took the picture on 30 June 1993.' (*Geoff Warburton*)

'I took this picture of David Powell, selling scratchins, 50p a bag, on 30 September 1990 at the Black Country Living Museum. I thought this scene was so typical of the nineteenth century!' (*Geoff Warburton*)

'Willenhall Primitive Methodist church choir, *c.* 1900. Methodism was very strong in the Black Country. These pictures show some of the Methodists in the choir and also how elaborate harvest festival could be.' (*K. Hunt*)

'This is Willenhall Primitive Methodist church and I think it is pre-1914.' (*K. Hunt*)

'Russell Street Primitive Methodist church, Willenhall, harvest festival, 1905.' (*K. Hunt*)

'I think this harvest festival at Russell Street Primitive Methodist church dates from the 1930s.' (*K. Hunt*)

'Wordsley church sits up well in my picture taken in 1988. Holy Trinity has a commanding view of its surroundings and is clear on the horizon from all around. Consecrated in 1831 and parish church of Kingswinford until 1846, it was restored in 1977 and 1981 with strong steel reinforcing bands around the tower to correct damage resulting from subsidence. Especially interesting for me is the tomb of John Northwood, surmounted by a copy of the Portland Vase which he managed to create at Wordsley, 1873–6.' (*Geoff Warburton*)

Frederick Onions (right) and Bill Poole (left) celebrating sixty years of lay preaching. (*Mrs D. Capewell*)

Frederick Onions (front row, left) with his 'Wesley' Football team, otherwise known as 'The Cobblers'. (*Mrs D. Capewell*)

'This is the Riddings Lane Bible Class Football Club in 1915–16 from Darlaston or Wednesbury. The President was A.E. Griffiths and the Honorary Secretary was W.T. Cartwright.' (*Mrs G. Holmes*)

Spring Head Methodist school room, 21 May 1995. (*Mary & Ted Evans*)

'Quarry Bank church on 28 April 1995. It was built of refractory bricks. These are resistant to very high temperatures and are good for kilns.' (*Geoff Warburton*)

'This is Wednesbury church. It is not only very old itself, but I have been told it is built inside a prehistoric rampart. Inside there is a fighting cock for a lectern.' (*Mrs Barbara Wakelin*)

'This is a picture from my family archives of Shelfield Senior School domestic science class, December 1935.' (*Terry Harrison*)

['My] mother is in this picture of the Red Cross Street sewing class, Wolverhampton, 1923/4.' (*Mrs M. Wilde*)

'This was my class at Slater Street School, Darlaston, *c.* 1956. The school stood across the road from the baths, but while the baths have been replaced by a new baths complex, the school has gone.' (*Bren Speed*)

'This is a picture of our local Tividale church nave, which has now been demolished.' (*Mrs Garrington*)

'St James' School and vicarage, Wednesbury, which I photographed on 25 March 1992. The church and school date from 1844 and the rectory from 1849, with restoration carried out by the Black Country Development Corporation. The pop group Slade performed here.' (*Geoff Warburton*)

'This is a picture of local Scouts, *c.* 1915, with my grandfather, Charlie Finch. The man on the right of the front row appears to be a member of the Boys' Brigade.' (*Mrs G. Holmes*)

'I think these Girl Guides are outside Darlaston Town Hall in the 1920s.' (*Mrs M. Harper*)

'A Business Tourism presentation was held at the Copthorne Hotel, Merry Hill, in September 1996. Left to right: Keith Cheetham (Director Black Country Tourism), Cllr Geoff Jewkes, Viv Astling, Cllr John Simpson (Mayor of Dudley), John Woodall, Cllr Fred Hunt.' (*Keith Cheetham*)

'The deal is struck in October 1994! Keith Cheetham shakes hands with Giorgio Perini from Italy on clinching a deal for a summer school for Italian students. Looking on is William Wilson, student accommodation officer, University of Wolverhampton.' (*Keith Cheetham*)

'A friendly guide on the Dudley Ghost Walk, which was set up by Black Country Tourism in 1974.' (*Keith Cheetham*)

'David Middleton of Black Country Tourism visiting Brierly Hill, Nanaimo, Vancouver Island, Canada. Black Country miners had gone to Canada to set up mines in Nanaimo in November 1854.' (*Keith Cheetham*)

Advertising Walsall. The first British large model aircraft, the Taylorcraft Auster with 100cc Aspera engine, being used for banner towing.' (*Jim Shelley*)

'John MacGregor Education Secretary visited Dudley College of Technology Business Centre in 1981. Left to right: Peter O'Brien, John MacGregor, Dr John Blackman MP (Dudley West).' (*Peter O'Brien*)

The unveiling of the Lone Rider motorcycle statue, 31 August 1996, at Safeway, Graiseley. AJS had been founded by the Stevens brothers and existed from 1914 to 1981. Geoffrey Stevens is in the centre, Jim Boulton is by the railing and the sculptor Robert Bowers, is on the left.' (*Geoff Warburton*)

A group from the Black Country Society on 8 June 1994 at Wolverhampton 21 Locks looking from Top Lock to Chubb Bridge and South to Broad Street to the site of the Canal Street Bridge which is now at the Black Country Living Museum.' (*Geoff Warburton*)

'This is a Steel Nut & Joseph Hampton works outing in the late 1920s, judging from the solid tyres. The firm was known as the "woden works", and the charabanc is probably standing in All Saints Road, Darlaston. My father, Leslie, is third from the right.' (*Bren Speed*)

'This shows Mr and Mrs W.H. Pennell, *c.* 1920, outside their home which was Maple House, Hatherton Street, Walsall. The property was demolished in about 1939, after a 100 year lease, to erect Kennings Garage, which itself became an arts centre for a short time. Mr and Mrs Pennell are my grandparents.' (*Mrs Kathleen Baldwin*)

'This is Bradley Hall, formerly of Kingswinford, prior to its dismantling by Major Kenneth Hutchinson Smith and re-erection in Stratford-upon-Avon, where it was sold for £2,000. According to Ron Davies' recent book, *One Man's Dream*, it has been valued recently at £1 million.' (*Geoff Warburton*)

'This was Emma Moseley's tobacconist's shop, 2 Caldmore Road, now known as Little Caldmore Road, where Henry Moseley had set up in business in 1882. This picture was taken soon after his widow Emma's death in 1926 and shows Frank Richardson in the doorway. He married her daughter Sal soon after Emma's death.' (*John Griffiths*)

'Stourton Castle began life as a Royal Hunting Lodge, probably in the eleventh century when it is reputed that William II was in Kinver. Since then it has had links with Henry II, John, Edward IV, Henry VII and Henry VIII. Cardinal Pole was born there in 1500. I took this photograph on 3 March 1991.' (*Geoff Warburton*)

Himley Hall on 25 March 1990 with a fine display of daffodils in the foreground. This was one of the Earl of Dudley's family homes and dates from the first half of the eighteenth century.' (*Geoff Warburton*)

Peter Wright says, 'This is a group of former Garringtons' employees in the Evergreen Room. Left to right: a former heat treatment worker(?), George Amos, Eric Rich (Assistant Works Manager), Harry Antill (Works Manager).' (*Garry Ashford-Smith*)

'Garringtons' Forty-Year Club was described by the late Lord Brookes as having been "informally established during the war years and formally soon afterwards. It embraces all men, working or retired, who have served for forty years. The annual Christmas dinner was at standards of a formal executive gathering, and for the long weekend summer outings – alternating between a British resort and a continental one not too distant or too expensive, was also set to achieve similar standards. Progressively there has emerged a company of men, whether labourers, craftsmen, technicians, managers or directors, who learned to be comfortable and relaxed with elegance and excellence. Joining members were properly presented with badges and other insignia of membership and I think, £40 in cash. . . . From the Forty-Year Club emerged the Evergreen Association at Garringtons and the Evergreen Room – a special Club Room at Darlaston, and from this the GKN Evergreen Association".' (*Garry Ashford-Smith*)

'These are local Scouts practising stretcher-bearing at camp, *c.* 1915. The Boys' Brigade officer is probably instructing the Scouts in First Aid. It looks as though he has a silver First Aid badge on his left sleeve from St John's Ambulance Brigade.' (*Mrs G. Holmes*)

Ned Williams regrets, 'The Pig on the Wall in Upper Gornal is about to close to be replaced by a McDonalds. Its name perpetuates the legend about "Who put the pig on the wall to watch the band go by?". Until 1985 the pub was the Bricklayers Arms, but the pig on the wall legend had became so strong in the Gornal area that a postcard had been produced illustrating the scene and listing possible suspects. It turns out not to be unique to Gornal; the same story is also known in other coalfield areas where every village knew their brass band was better than their neighbours'. (*Ned Williams*)

'My parents were on a motor bus outing in Weston-super-Mare before the Second World War and are sitting in the second row back. They were enjoying a short holiday away from Darlaston.' (*Bren Speed*)

Ken Proud, a lifelong supporter of Walsall Football Club, says, 'This is a very good picture of Bescot stadium taken by David Wilkins from the air. You can see the all-weather pitch to one side and there are plans for further car-parking. The Home Stand is going to be extended upwards. This is to provide seating instead of standing room now that the club is in Division One. It will increase capacity from 9,500 to 10,000.' (*David Wilkins at First House Photography*)

'This is a full house crowd, standing shoulder-to-shoulder at Walsall's Fellows Park in the 1930s'. (*Tony Matthews*)

'This is Walsall Football Club in 1912. It turned up in my family archives, but I don't know much more about it.' (*Terry Harrison*)

'This is a postwar picture of Walsall Football Club Supporters Club, *c.* 1955/6.' (*Terry Harrison*)

Tony Matthews says, 'This is the Hawthorns, West Bromwich Football Club's stadium photographed from the air by David Wilkins. The team are sometimes known as "The Throstles" and Bob Bibby discusses the origin of the term in his *Grey Paes & Bacon*. "After playing in a variety of grounds in the early part of their life, the club moved to its present ground, The Hawthorns, in 1900. The ground then was largely common land with many hawthorn bushes that attracted large numbers of song-thrushes, otherwise known as throstles. . . . Their ground is the highest in Britain, being some 550 feet above sea level".' (*David Wilkins at First House Photography*)

'West Bromwich Albion on 3 September 1900 at their new ground, the Hawthorns, where they are still based.' (*Tony Matthews*)

'This is the Old Woodman Inn as it was when the Albion went to the Hawthorns in 1900.' (*Tony Matthews*)

'This postcard from about 1910 shows the West Bromwich Albion Football Club Hawthorns ground on the left of Halford's Lane. They had moved here from Stoney Lane in 1900.' (*Tony Matthews*)

'This is the front cover of the *Albion News*, published on 2 September 1905. It contains an account of W. Barber, the team's trainer, who had first played for the club in 1886–7. Albion had won the English Cup in 1888 and 1892.' (*Tony Matthews*)

This picture of Molineux stadium, Wolverhampton has been taken from the air at the club's 125th anniversary. As Sir Jack Hayward wrote in the *Express & Star* on 25 October, 'Today we celebrate the 125th anniversary of the founding of this great club – Wolverhampton Wanderers. A club that was one of the 12 founder members of the Football League. . . . This is the club of Billy Wright, Stan Cullis, Ron Flowers, Bill Slater, Bert Williams, Peter Broadbent, Mullen and Hancocks, John Richards, Steve Bull and so many other great names.' (*David Wilkins at First House Photography*)

FOOTBALL.

THE FIRST

GENERAL MEETING

OF THE

GOLDTHORN

FOOTBALL CLUB

Will (by the kind permission of the Vicar) be held at

ST. LUKE'S SCHOOL,

BLAKENHALL,

ON

Friday next, November 10, 1876,

AT 7.30 P.M.

Any Gentleman interested in the game is invited to attend.

'I have already published this poster advertising the first General Meeting of the Goldthorn Football Club in 1876 in *The Wolves Story*. Wolverhampton Wanderers owe their inception to the enthusiasm of a band of scholars and choristers. Four months later John Baynton and John Brodie were pupil-teachers at St Luke's School, Blakenhall, when John Addenbrooke, a young teacher there, was a member of St Luke's Junior Football Team. Some St Luke's footballers also played cricket for the Blakenhall Wanderers Cricket Club. Shortly after 1880 the two clubs amalgamated, leading eventually to the name Wolverhampton Wanderers Football Club. Goldthorn FC appears to have been an early, temporary name.' (*Tony Matthews*)

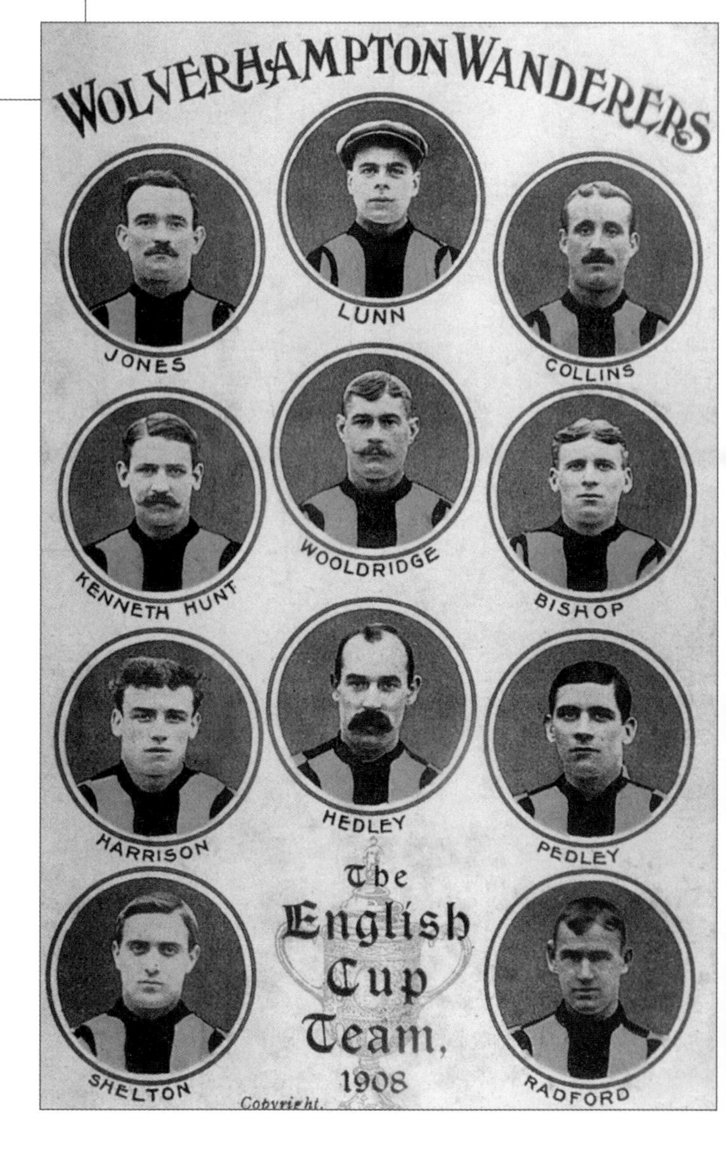

The Wolverhampton Wanderers team which won the English Cup in 1908. (*Tony Matthews*)

The Wolverhampton Wanderers programme for their match against Moscow Dynamo in Molineux's centenary year, 1989. As Geoff Allman recalls, 'Wolves won 3–2, Bull 2, Dennison 1. In previous matches Wolves beat Dynamo on 9 November 1955 2–1, but lost to Dynamo 4–2 on 8 March 1982.' (*Tony Matthews*)

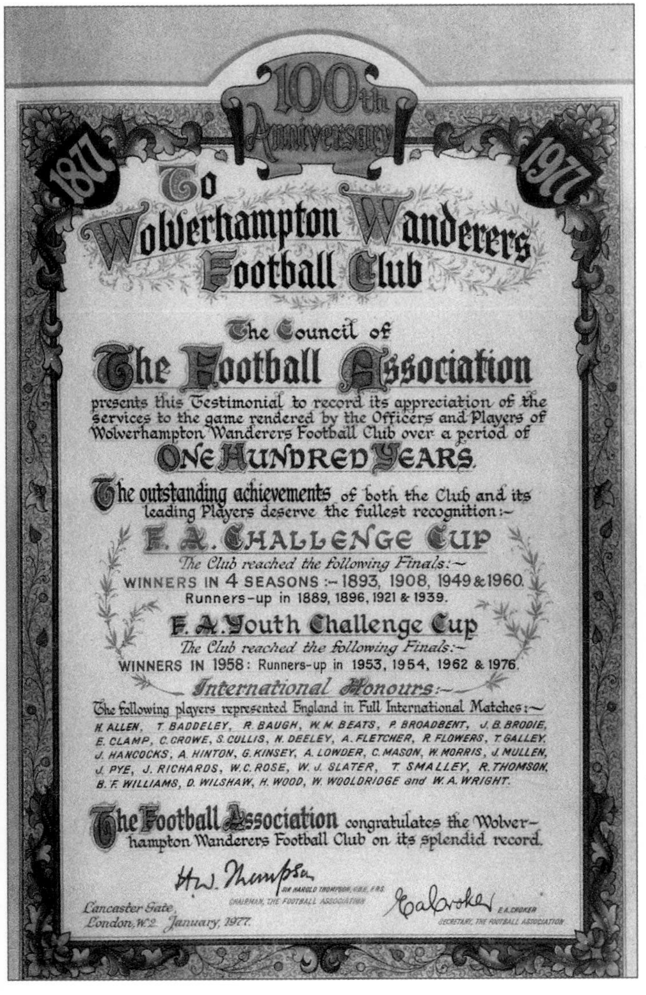

100th Anniversary

1877 1977

To Wolverhampton Wanderers Football Club

The Council of The Football Association presents this Testimonial to record its appreciation of the services to the game rendered by the Officers and Players of Wolverhampton Wanderers Football Club over a period of

ONE HUNDRED YEARS.

The outstanding achievements of both the Club and its leading Players deserve the fullest recognition:–

F. A. CHALLENGE CUP

The Club reached the following Finals:–

WINNERS IN 4 SEASONS:– 1893, 1908, 1949 & 1960.

Runners-up in 1889, 1896, 1921 & 1939.

F. A. Youth Challenge Cup

The Club reached the following Finals:–

WINNERS IN 1958: Runners-up in 1953, 1954, 1962 & 1976.

International Honours:–

The following players represented England in Full International Matches:–

H. ALLEN, T. BADDELEY, R. BAUGH, W. M. BEATS, P. BROADBENT, J. B. BRODIE, E. CLAMP, C. CROWE, S. CULLIS, N. DEELEY, A. FLETCHER, R. FLOWERS, T. GALLEY, J. HANCOCKS, A. HINTON, G. KINSEY, A. LOWDER, C. MASON, W. MORRIS, J. MULLEN, J. PYE, J. RICHARDS, W. C. ROSE, W. J. SLATER, T. SMALLEY, R. THOMSON, B. F. WILLIAMS, D. WILSHAW, H. WOOD, W. WOOLDRIDGE and W. A. WRIGHT.

The Football Association congratulates the Wolverhampton Wanderers Football Club on its splendid record.

H. W. Thompson
SIR HAROLD THOMPSON, C.B.E., F.R.S.
CHAIRMAN, THE FOOTBALL ASSOCIATION

E. A. Croker
E. A. CROKER
SECRETARY, THE FOOTBALL ASSOCIATION

Lancaster Gate,
London, W.2. January, 1977.

The Football Association Testimonial for Wolverhampton Wanderers' 100 years in 1977, recording that they had won the cup four times and been finalists in a further four matches. (*Tony Matthews*)

'I found this picture of Rushall Olympic FC 1952/3 and the next one of 1919/20 when I embarked on family history.' (*Terry Harrison*)

'This is Rushall Olympic FC 1919/20. (*Terry Harrison*)

'Bloxwich Hockey Club 1st XI 1921/2. Back: ? Wilkes, Jim Smith, Bill Styles, ? Rowbottom, "Dinky" Ray Wilkes, Reg Wilkes. Front: Joe Smith, Fred Shortman, Harry Wootton, Leonard Ross, George Herbert.' (*Mrs M. Wootton*)

'This is Darlaston Football Club in the 1971/2 season. In those days I was quite keen on the local club because I had a cousin, Malcolm Shinton, who used to play for them. He used to live in Wednesbury and was actually offered a trial with Wolves, but in the end he didn't take it up.' (*Mrs Maureen Vodden*)

'It wasn't all work and no play at F.H. Lloyds. This shows apprentices playing "football" in 1958!' (*Fred Parker*)

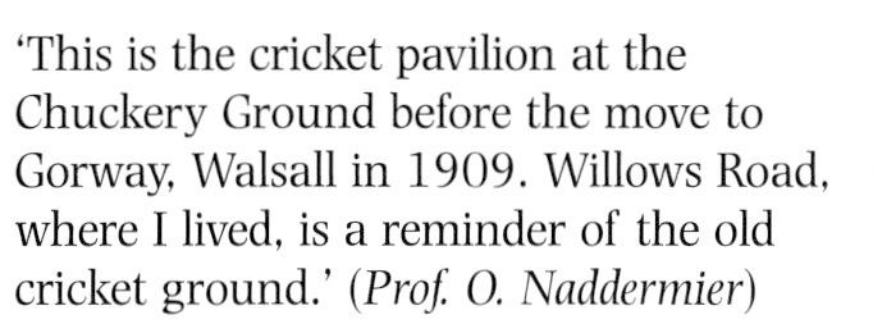

'This is the cricket pavilion at the Chuckery Ground before the move to Gorway, Walsall in 1909. Willows Road, where I lived, is a reminder of the old cricket ground.' (*Prof. O. Naddermier*)

'This is Walsall Athletic Club, 1956/7, cross country section. Back row, left to right: Me (Alan Newman), Tom Moore, -?-, D. Humpage, -?-. Front row: -?-, Don Greaves, John Tucker, -?-. As it's some time ago, I can't remember all the names.' (*Alan Newman*)

'Wednesbury Old Athletic Football Club in 1877. This is among the family archives, because, although we are established in Walsall, our family came originally from Wednesbury and my father and grandfather had maintained the links by continuing membership of sports clubs over there.' (*Martin Skidmore*)

'Many years ago I took this picture of boys fishing in the canal. It is still a typical sport in the Black Country.' (*Terry Harrison*)

'Quite a crowd turned up for the unveiling of a memorial to William Perry, the "Tipton Slasher" on 3 May 1993. This stands in the Coronation Gardens, Owen Street. Tony Maycock, TV reporter, is in the centre.' (*Ian Bott*)

'Willenhall Police FC, 1958/9, which took part in the Chief Constable's Cup Final. We were pictured on Palethorpes' Ground at Tipton and I am first left on the back row. I went on to Aldridge as a sergeant and when I retired in 1980, as an officer of St John Ambulance, I went to British Gas to run their First Aid.' (*E. Knight*)

Darlington Street Methodist church, 6 March 1992. 'The church was built in 1900/1. The architect was Arthur Marshall II. Nikolaus Pevsner described it as "a very uncommon kind of design for the purpose". Darlington Street had been built in the early 1820s as part of the London–Tettenhall–Holyhead Road.' (*Geoff Warburton*)

'This is the Old Swan, Netherton, 16 September 1990, which was better known as "Ma Pardoe's".' (*Geoff Warburton*)

The Bottle & Glass pub is now re-erected at the Black Country Living Museum. This shows it before dismantling. Stan Hill remembers it from his boyhood, 'Like the poet Seamus Heaney, who as a child followed his father behind the plough in Northern Ireland, when I was about eight years old in the 1930s during school holidays I followed my father on his "walk" as a postman in Brierley Hill. Sometimes he delivered around Brockmoor on the edge of the postal district. On one occasion he had a packet for the licensee of the Bottle & Glass Inn which backed on to the Stourbridge Canal at Buckpool. On arrival he told me to sit on the step while he made the delivery. Shortly afterwards he re-appeared wiping his hand across his lips and said, "Don't tell your mother I went in there".' (*BCLM Collection*)

7

People of the Black Country

Margaret Allen, former headmistress of Hall Green Infants' School, remembers dressing up for this picture when she posed at Firkins Bakery, West Bromwich, to sell her famous lardy (dripping) cakes in September 1985 to promote the Black Country Living Museum. She was a founder member of the Friends of the Museum and is now a vice-president. (*Mrs M. Allen*)

'Arthur Farrington took this picture of an unknown worker at Eylands in the early 1900s. It is one of the finest portraits of a working man that I think you will see. He was employed in the heat treatment shop. Buckles were first placed in the tubs shown in the photograph and then put in the oven, heated to a high temperature and then allowed to cool slowly. This treatment prevented the buckles from becoming brittle.' (*John Griffiths*)

'This picture of a mother and her children outside her cottage must be before the First World War. I don't know who they were, but R. White's Lemonade advertised on the wall was well known for years.' (*E.D. Freeth*)

'Lord Peter Archer of Sandwell launches the Black Country Conference Manual in 1994.' (*Keith Cheetham*)

Bill Bailey is seen in the 1970s making gear levers for Minis. His brother George also worked on Bradley hammers at Garringtons. Peter Wright recalls the regular 'tap, tap, tap' as they were forged. He used to drive a 3-ton truck load of the forgings to Clevedon, the other side of Bristol, where they were drawn out and then delivered to Austin's assembly line, Birmingham. (*Garry Ashford-Smith*)

'This is our grandfather, Harry Bednall, in his office in Eldon Street, Walsall. The picture was taken by our uncle, J.A. Stone, who is Rex Stone's father. Harry Bednall changed from saddlery to leather clothing for motor cyclists and motorists. In the Second World War he turned to war work and made leather clothing for air crew.' (*Nancy & Mary Sankey*)

'This shows me driving a six-wheeler lorry for Wheway Watsons, carrying the last load of chain made of Herc Alloy for an order in Reykjavik in 1972. The people who made it are sitting on the back and I think it's a couple of salesmen who are standing by the cab.' (*B. Benton*)

'My father, Herbert Bird, is on the extreme right and Arthur May, a family friend, is second from the left. Father was always ready to have a go and join in whether he could play the game or not. The tennis court is probably West Smethwick Park.' (*Mrs Margaret Wootton*)

'This is my mother and father, Herbert Bird and Eva, née Perry, out for the day in a Buick(?) probably before they were married in the 1920s.' (*Mrs Margaret Wootton*)

'Irving Bosco, alias William Bainton, born at Keighley in Yorkshire. His claim to fame is to have opened the first cinema in the Black Country in 1909, well before the Kinematograph Act came into force on 1 January 1910, thus beginning the history of "proper" cinemas. He also showed films at the Palace in West Bromwich before the Act of 1910. Later it became The Queens. After the war Mr Bosco felt uncertain of the industry's future and put his cinemas up for sale in 1920.' (*Ned Williams*)

'Sculptor Robert Bowers (left), a former pupil of mine at Kates Hill Primary School, Dudley, 1975–86, and me (right). This was the week after my triple bypass operation.' (*Geoff Warburton*)

Walsall Enterprise Agency, at a meeting of Willenhall Breakfast Business Club, 1994. Left to right, Bruce Biddle, Midland Bank, the speaker, Cllr Mike Bird, Reg Wrighton, chairman, Peter O'Brien.' (*D.F. Vodden*)

'My father, J. Bristow, is shown with the 'bump test' machine he developed in his small factory in our backyard for testing car radios in the very early 1950s. In the early days of car radios, problems were encountered with reception because of the rattle and bumps old cars were renowned for. This machine gave a strenuous test to the radios, which were fixed to the flat top of the machine. When it was switched on, it would shake and vibrate the radio far worse than any road. I'm not sure who this machine was made for as I was only eleven or twelve at the time, but I think it could have been RGD, who were based near Bridgnorth, and used to make TVs and radios after the war and eventually became Decca, so I believe. After my father's early death my brothers carried on the business until the end of the 1970s.' (*R. Bristow*)

Lord and Lady Brookes with his portrait in the Evergreen Room, Garringtons, Darlaston. Peter Wright, who used to act as chauffeur, remembers them both as being keen fishermen and making full use of GKN's cottage on the Wye at Rhayader. He often drove Lady Brookes to the shops in Wednesbury and remembers how her mother had kept a very large pub in the High Street there in a good old-fashioned way. (*Garry Ashford-Smith*)

The Evergreen Room

Its Origin and formation

At a time when Mr. R. P. Brookes* (later to become Lord Brookes) was Chairman of Garringtons Limited he made frequent journeys from the Bromsgrove factory to the works at Darlaston. On one such occasion, during the summer of 1960, when travelling through the town centre, he was saddened by the sight of some twenty or more elderly men, sitting on a low wall, gazing aimlessly about them. Many, he learned, were old employees of Garringtons who had ceased active work.

From then on he resolved that those who had spent the best years of their lives in the service of his Company should be given a continued purpose and feeling of still belonging. Thus the Evergreen Room came into being, specially built and equipped for the exclusive use of retired long service personnel and available daily for companionship, relaxation and refreshment. He performed the official opening on the 24th February 1961.

* He became GKN Group Chairman in 1965, was Knighted in 1971, and on his retirement in 1975, was made GKN Life President. In the same year he was created a Life Peer with the title – Baron Brookes of West Bromwich.

Garringtons' Evergreen Room notice. (*Garry Ashford-Smith*)

'Ned Williams heads a Black Country Society walk at Pat Collins' grave in Bloxwich Cemetery on 14 June 1995. He is buried here with his second wife, Clara. His first wife died in 1933 and is buried at Wrexham, and Pat Collins has a memorial there, too. Among the group can be seen Ned Williams, Malcolm Lacy, Alex Chatwin, Tony ?, Freda Allen and Bob Hyde.' (*Geoff Warburton*)

'This is the Revd D.C. Cooper, of Russell Street Primitive Methodist church, Willenhall, *c.* 1905.' (*K. Hunt*)

'This is a man I admire very much, Father James Curtin, parish priest of St Thomas of Canterbury, Coalpool, who won £100,000 on the pools and gave it all away apart from buying himself a Mini car. Most of the money went to the IBROX Disaster Fund.' (*Peter O'Brien*)

Peter Wright remembers Ben Dangerfield who is seen here shaping out a component part for the car industry in Shop 70, Darlaston in 1931. The floor is covered in sawdust to absorb the scale from the forgings. There was a large family of Dangerfields and most of them worked at Garringtons. (*Garry Ashford-Smith*)

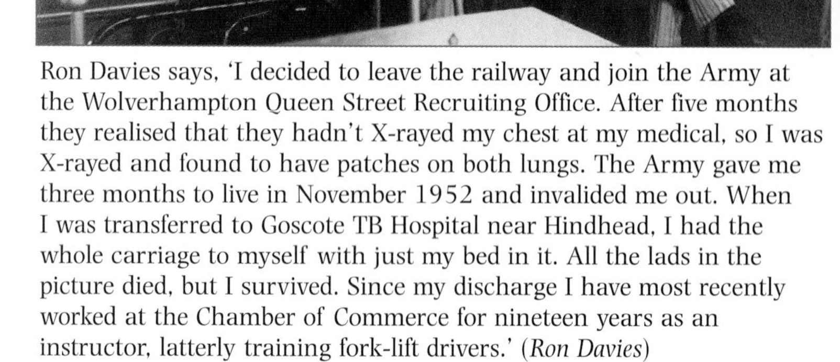

Ron Davies says, 'I decided to leave the railway and join the Army at the Wolverhampton Queen Street Recruiting Office. After five months they realised that they hadn't X-rayed my chest at my medical, so I was X-rayed and found to have patches on both lungs. The Army gave me three months to live in November 1952 and invalided me out. When I was transferred to Goscote TB Hospital near Hindhead, I had the whole carriage to myself with just my bed in it. All the lads in the picture died, but I survived. Since my discharge I have most recently worked at the Chamber of Commerce for nineteen years as an instructor, latterly training fork-lift drivers.' (*Ron Davies*)

'I am at the bottom of Walsall Market in 1953 with Frank Davies and Norman, an amateur boxer.' (*Ron Davies*)

'The Revd Jack Davies, vicar of All Saints', Darlaston, parading in the early 1960s. I think it is in Bull Piece. On his right is Len Bailey, a local photographer, and on his left is Ted Malpass, who was a builder. They were both churchwardens.' (*Bren Speed*)

'This is retired Superintendent Joe Davies dressed as a constable in uniform of the Wolverhampton force prior to the 1960s. He has his cape on the bicycle and on his left arm sports the St John's First Aid badge. He is seen chatting to Knox Mackay and Blue.' Roy Meller adds, 'He served first in the Wolverhampton police before joining the West Midlands Force where he served in the Traffic Division.' (*Geoff Warburton*)

'This is the 3rd Earl of Dudley's grave at Himley, 13 June 1992. Eric Ward was born on 30 January 1894 and died on 26 December 1969 in France and was buried there originally. The blue brick path was specially laid and his much younger third wife had a plot reserved for her. Ivy and rosemary had been planted in the 1930s.' (*Geoff Warburton*)

The late J.L. (Jim) Edwards says, 'The Earl of Dudley and I are in Pitts Cott at the Black Country Living Museum. It was the day of the official opening of this building and I am explaining to him that I had donated the spelter ornaments on the mantelpiece. They are inscribed "La Pouvoir" and "La Force" and originally belonged to my late mother-in-law, Mrs Lillian Duncan, who lived to the ripe old age of ninety-seven.' (*Rosemary Corns*)

'Duncan Edwards' grave is in the Stourbridge Road Cemetery, Dudley. Bob Bibby referred to him in *Grey Paes and Bacon* as: "one of the famous Busby babes so tragically killed in the Munich airport crash of 1958. Edwards was born in Dudley and was an outstanding schoolboy footballer, playing for the England Schoolboys team at the age of only thirteen. At 16 he signed for Manchester United. . . . Two years later, at the age of 18, he was picked for England at left half against Scotland – England's youngest ever player." I also wrote him up in a book in 1986, and took this picture on 19 December 1990.' (*Geoff Warburton*)

'This picture of three generations of the Everton family dates from the 1920s. On the extreme right is my grandfather, Eli, who was originally apprenticed as a wheelwright in 1871 to Edward Preece from Chaddesley Corbett and eventually developed his skills as a coachbuilder in Blackheath.' (*R. Everton*)

This Indenture Witnesseth:

That *Eli Everton* a poor Boy of the Parish of CHADDESLEY CORBETT, in the County of Worcester, as well of his own free Will, as also by and with the approbation of WILLIAM PIPPET, of COUGHTON, in the County of Warwick, Gentleman, agent to SIR NICHOLAS W. G. THROCKMORTON, of BUCKLAND, in the County of Berkshire, Baronet, doth put himself Apprentice to *Edward Preece* of the Parish of *Rowley Regis* in the County of *Stafford* to learn his Art; and with him, after the manner of an Apprentice, to serve from the Day of the Date hereof, until he attain the age of Twenty-one Years, and fully to be complete and ended; during which Term the said Apprentice his Master faithfully shall and will serve, his Secrets keep, his lawful Commands every where gladly do; he shall do no Damage to his said Master, nor see it done of others, but to his power shall let or forthwith give Notice to his said Master, of the same; ~~the Goods of his said Master he shall~~ not waste, nor the same without License of him to any give or lend: Hurt to his Master he shall not do, cause, or procure to be done; he shall neither Buy nor Sell without his Master's License; Taverns, Inns, or Alehouses, he shall not haunt; at Cards, Dice, Tables, or any other unlawful Game, he shall not play; Matrimony he shall not contract during the said Term, nor from the service of his said Master Day or Night absent himself, but in all Things as a faithful and honest Apprentice shall and will demean and behave himself towards his said Master and all his during the said Term.

And the said *Edward Preece* in Consideration of the Sum of Twelve Pounds, to be paid him as hereinafter mentioned (that is to say), the Sum of Six Pounds, part thereof, at the Time of executing these Presents, and the further Sum of Six Pounds when and as soon as the said Apprentice shall have served Half his Time (the same being Charity Money left for placing poor Children Apprentice, Inhabitants of Chaddesley Corbett aforesaid, by Dame MARY YATE, late of *1873 Jan* Harvington Hall, in the said Parish of Chaddesley Corbett, Widow, deceased;) the said Apprentice in the Art of *Wheelwright and Carpenter* which he now useth, shall teach and instruct, or cause to be taught and instructed, in the best Way and Manner that he can, finding and allowing, unto his said Apprentice, sufficient Meat, Drink, Clothes, Washing, Lodging, and all other Necessaries during the said Term. And also shall and will, at the end of the said Term, allow and give unto the said Apprentice one good new suit of Apparel. And for the true performance of all and every the Covenants and Agreements aforesaid, either of the said parties bindeth himself and themselves firmly by these Presents. *IN WITNESS* whereof the Parties first above named to these present Indentures have interchangeably put their Hands and Seals the *Thirty fifth* Year of the Reign of Our Sovereign Lady Victoria the First, by the Grace of God of the United Kingdom of Great Britain and Ireland Queen, Defender of the Faith, &c., and in the Year of Our Lord One Thousand Eight Hundred and *Twentyone*

[illegible] Eli Everton

Signed, sealed, and delivered in the presence of *[illegible] Pippet* — *Edward Preece*

Received this *Twelfth* *day of January, 18*70 *the Sum of Six Pounds, being the First Moiety within mentioned to be paid to me.*

E Preece

Received this *fifteenth* *day of January, 18____ the Sum of Six Pounds, being the Second Moiety within mentioned to be paid to me.*

[illegible] W Pippet Jan 15 - 1876 — *[illegible] Preece*

Indenture for Eli Everton, 1871. (*R. Everton*)

Robert Everton with a Richardson Brothers' lorry at the Three Counties' Show, Malvern, 1960s. He said, 'We were coachbuilders and had painted the current prime minister's name and address on the cab doors as a joke, which certainly attracted a lot of interest, both at the show and travelling up and down the motorway!' (*R. Everton*)

'Eylands' electroplating shop, Lower Rushall Street, Walsall, photographed by one of the Farrington brothers in the early 1900s.' (*John Griffiths*)

'James Foster-Smith was managing director of Wellman Smith Owen Engineering Ltd. He died on 24 January 1947. The firm, like many others in the Black Country, had carried out a lot of work for the war effort.' (*Mrs G. Holmes*)

'I took this group at the unveiling of the AJS Memorial on 31 August 1996. Centre, left to right: Steve Field, Robert Bowers (sculptor), Geoff Stevens.' (*Geoff Warburton*)

George Garratt, hammer forge foreman, and Lord Brookes examining radius rod arms produced on the Beche hammers. This was probably his last visit to Darlaston. Lord Brookes died on the Isle of Man in August 2002. Peter Wright says, 'George Garratt, a keen fisherman, still lives in Coalpool, Walsall.' (*Garry Ashford-Smith*)

'John Garrington, founder of Garringtons, pictured in his prime, had started his business in 1837 in a small way as a blacksmith at St Catherine's Cross near Darlaston when he was thirty-nine. In 1840 he opened his first factory, calling it the Albert Works to mark Queen Victoria's wedding. The workshop contained about a dozen hammers varying from 2 cwt to 20 cwt, a few stripping presses and a tool room employing six people. It also had one lathe, one drilling machine, one planer and one shaper. Almost 90 per cent of the business was forgings for the tube trade, but he also made forgings for tools such as hammers, pliers, pincers, screwdrivers. From the outset John had kept his workers by paying them £1 a week when the standard wage for a trained labourer's fifty-four-hour week was 18*s*.' (*Garry Ashford-Smith*)

'John Garrington looks more elderly in this picture. He was to die at seventy-nine. His business was divided equally among the surviving members of his family and carried on by his sons Richard and Benjamin.' (*Garry Ashford-Smith*)

'Albert (Bert) Garrington inherited the business in 1907 on his father Richard's death. In 1911 Garringtons was acquired by F.W. Cotterill Ltd, who then amalgamated with Guest Keen and Nettlefold Ltd (later GKN). In 1912 John Garrington and Sons Ltd was registered as a private limited company. Production at this time was 600 tons of forgings per annum.' (*Garry Ashford-Smith*)

'This is F.J.J. Gibbons, MD of Gibbons in the 1940s, the oldest firm of lock makers in UK, which had been established in Wolverhampton in about 1680 by Thomas Gibbons. The site of the former very large works is occupied by Courts in the Melbourne Street area. After being sold to Radiation then taken over by TI, and after the closing of the Wolverhampton site, some of Gibbons' lock makers went to Willenhall.' (*Albert Benbow*)

'Walter Gregory (left) was the commercial manager of Rubery Owen at Darlaston and eventually went to Australia. Ray Hancox was managing director of Rubery Owen Steelwork. Here they are examining a model of the multi-storey car park for Worcester.' (*Ted Hickinbottom*)

'George Higginson, Thomas Harding and his sons Eddie, me, and Alf, on the Dingley Road allotments in 1946 or 1947. Mr Higginson was a moulder at F.H. Lloyd and my father was a carpenter and joiner. Dingley Road allotments had just been developed from the "Cow Field" as I knew it; they had been previously rented out to a Mr Hubble who had a butcher's business in Bilston and used to run cows and sheep here. I don't know whether Wednesbury Council owned this ground or whether it was F.H. Lloyds'. Certainly F.H. Lloyds owned all the ground in the rear of this photograph right back to Wood Green. The Wood Green railway station can be seen on the left-hand side on the horizon.' (*Eddie Harding*)

'I was a crane driver at Talbot Steads, although I started there at fourteen in 1943, defrazing tubes. At fifteen I was grinding tools, when I was invited to operate a collett machine doing twelve-hour night shifts. That wouldn't be allowed today. In this picture I am standing beside Bill who is on a jig boring in the toolroom. After National Service in the RAF I came back in 1949 and was soon transferred to CTP (continual tube production). The firm changed from Talbot Steads to Tube Investments about then. After a spell in the tool room I was put on crane driving, then on to a Herbert No. 19 lathe. I was made redundant in 1973, but finished my working life at Crabtree's as a patrol inspector, from which I was made redundant in 1991.' (*Len Harrison*)

'Lieutenant Corporal John H. Harrison of the Royal Engineers with his wife Amelia, whom he married during the First World War. After demob he worked as a riveter at Horsley Piggotts, near Tipton, where he rose to foreman.' (*Terry Harrison*)

H.G. Hawley, grandson of the founder of the Walsall firm Hawley's Leathergoods. (*Miss Lillian Hawley*)

This is a picture of my husband, Stan Hemminsley, having a tea break in his early working days in a foundry. (*Mrs B. Hemminsley*)

'This is my father, George Hunt, locksmith and owner of a locksworks, second left in the back row, *c.* 1926. He retired in 1949 aged seventy! On his left is his niece, Alice Holt, and far right is Tom Holt his brother-in-law. George Hunt operated as a locksmith in Orchard Road, Willenhall.' (*K. Hunt*)

'Albert Edward Hill was my father, seen here in postman's uniform. He had served in the Royal Engineers in the First World War and, as a result of being gassed, was advised to take an outdoor job which led to his becoming a postman until his retirement in 1950.' (*Stan Hill*)

'Before the Stourbridge Rally in 1962 the government was planning to shut down hundreds of miles of the nation's canals, including part of the Staffordshire and Worcestershire, the Stourbridge and Dudley and making the Dudley and Netherton tunnels redundant. Canal enthusiasts forced the government to back down in August 1962. The picture shows David Hutchings and committee members using a Tilley lamp, a thunderstorm having knocked out the site's electricity supply.' (*Alan Smith MBE*)

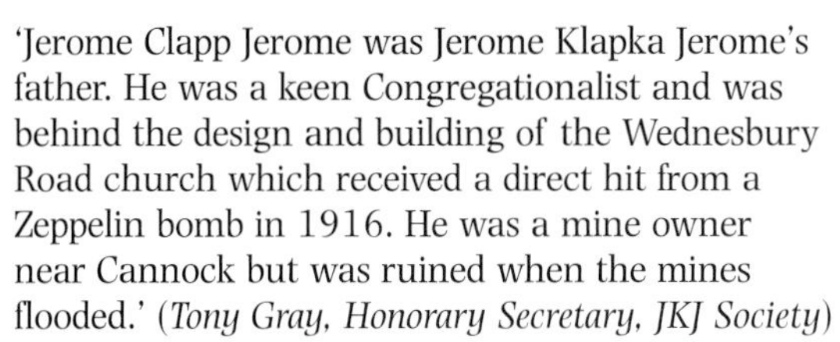

'Jerome Clapp Jerome was Jerome Klapka Jerome's father. He was a keen Congregationalist and was behind the design and building of the Wednesbury Road church which received a direct hit from a Zeppelin bomb in 1916. He was a mine owner near Cannock but was ruined when the mines flooded.' (*Tony Gray, Honorary Secretary, JKJ Society*)

'I have been given this picture of Jerome K. Jerome quite recently. I think it shows him in his late thirties. Although he left Walsall at the age of two, he has always been regarded as a son of the town and was invited back in 1927 to receive the Freedom of the Borough.' (*Tony Gray, Honorary Secretary, JKJ Society*)

Peter Wright says, 'These are Johnny Heath, Eric Rich and Tom Kirk. Behind them is a diagram of the Lasco Hammer Extrusion Press with an axle shaft drawing at Garringtons. Tom Kirk was very clever and a designer, and has now recovered from the effects of a stroke which he had at fifty. Eric Rich came to Darlaston from Bromsgrove where he had already made his name by standing up to the unions. By the time he retired he had become Works Manager. Johnny Heath stayed on to the end to oversee the completion of an important order for Ford Transit half shafts.' (*Garry Ashford-Smith*)

'Sir Keith Joseph gave a talk at the Victoria Hotel, Wolverhampton in 1978 about government wages policy. Left to right: Bill Leach (Chairman, Institute of Management), Ken Croxall (Institute of Purchasing and Supply), Peter O'Brien (Chairman, Institute of Works Managers), Sir Keith Joseph, Les Hartshorne (Chairman, Institute of Personnel Managers).' (*Peter O'Brien*)

The architect R.G. Madeley, in front of the former Savoy cinema, Park Street, Walsall, says, 'This was my first major project when I became a partner in Hickton & Madeley in 1936. The cinema was built on the awkwardly shaped site of the former Her Majesty's Theatre. The builder had started work before the final elevation drawings had been delivered so that some decorative detail on the side walls did not begin until about 10ft above the ground. It was officially opened in 1938 by the Mayor, Dr Drabble.' (*D.F. Vodden*)

'This is me, Anthea Mander, at Wightwick during probably the happiest period of my life. It was about this time that I was introduced to cultural activities such as music and art.' (*Anthea Mander*)

'Sir Stanley Matthews officially opens Walsall's new Bescot stadium on 18 August 1990 after they moved from Fellows Park. Left to right: Barry Blower (Chairman), Sir Stanley, the Mayoress and Mayor, Cllr Malcolm Barton.' (*Tony Matthews*)

'Bill McGarry was a former manager of Wolverhampton Wanderers who was employed to start a course in business management by Dudley College. Later I remember he emigrated to Zambia.' (*Peter O'Brien*)

'When Bob Millington starts restoring a vintage fire engine you know that the end result will be superb. He is seen here with his Leyland FK9 Cub pump escape DNP 721, which was supplied to the Borough of Stourbridge Fire Brigade in 1940.' (*R. Everton*)

John Griffiths, who published this picture in a calendar, says, 'William Moseley worked for Eyland & Sons from around 1918 until illness forced his retirement at the age of seventy in 1954. This picture is of his family in about 1890.' (*John Griffiths*)

'The Rubery Owen Works employed thousands and thousands of people at its height, engineering car parts for the West Midlands' automotive industry. Grace Owen presents a silver salver to Alderman Amery following the launch of automation at Rubery Owen, 14 October 1963.' (*Ted Hickinbottom*)

'My father-in-law, Horace Parke, getting through the floods near the Globe Inn and James Bridge, Darlaston Road, in the mid-1960s in his Morris Minor. The floods used to be bad in those days but you don't get much more than a large puddle now.' (*Barrie Benton*)

'Three workmen, two artists, one statue': *Pegasus* being erected. Left to right: Geoff Warburton, Steve Field (borough artist).' (*Ron Julian*)

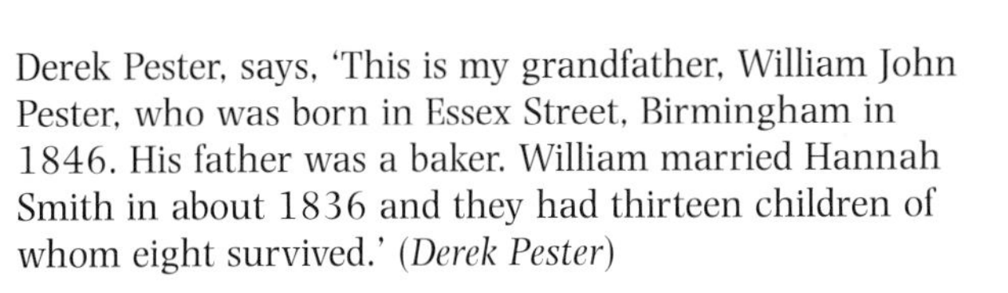

Derek Pester, says, 'This is my grandfather, William John Pester, who was born in Essex Street, Birmingham in 1846. His father was a baker. William married Hannah Smith in about 1836 and they had thirteen children of whom eight survived.' (*Derek Pester*)

'Lisa Potts was awarded the George Medal in the Birthday Honours List, June 1997, for service in saving the lives of a number of children from a man armed with a machete, despite being severely injured herself. While clearing away after a Teddy Bears' Picnic, Miss Potts, a nursery nurse, was in charge of a class of some twenty three-and-a-half to four-and-a-half year olds. . .'. Stan Hill was very critical of the Criminal Injuries Board's delay when he wrote of 'this brave young lady' in the December 2000 *Blackcountryman*. (*Stan Hill*)

'Arthur Reeves was Chance Brothers' furnace designer and engineer for fifty-two years. He died on 26 August 1995 aged ninety-three.' (*Geoff Warburton*)

'The Richardson twins at the launch of Stan Hill's *Brierley Hill and Story* on 23 November 1999 at the Copthorne Hotel. Roy and Don Richardson (left and centre) presenting me with a bottle of Dom Perignon champagne.' (*Stan Hill*)

Ian Walden, Black Country Living Museum Director, says, 'This shows a great friend of the museum, Sir David Rowe-Ham GBE, former Lord Mayor of the City of London, inaugurating the Transport Gallery at the Black Country Living Museum in 1995.' (*BCLM*)

Ian Walden says, 'This is a picture of Museum Chairman Jack Russell making a speech to Friends of the Black Country Museum and others at the ten-year celebrations of Trams at the Museum.' (*BCLM*)

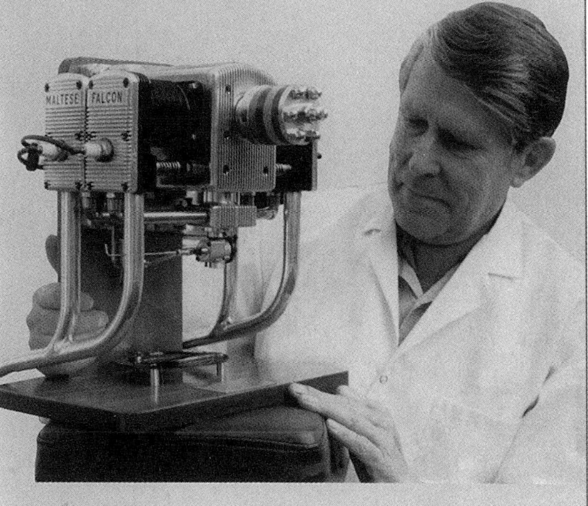

'For many years I have flown a 15ft wingspan Taylorcraft model plane using a 100cc Aspera (large Flymo) engine. This was sufficient for normal flying but inadequate to tow banners in a wind. In winter 1997 I decided to make an improved power plant which would drive a scale size prop at 2,000–3,000 rpm to give ample power, and look and sound right. The Maltese Falcon provides ample power for models up to 100lb in weight.' (*Jim Shelley*)

Jim Shelley's Frisco Jazz Band. Jim says, 'The band, with its emphasis on well-structured ensemble playing, follows the same path that the American Lu Watters trod earlier, and is almost wholly inspired by an enthusiasm for the giants of the '20s classic period. Tuesday 25 February 1986 saw the first outing of the band (after a whole 1¼ hours rehearsing!) at the Boundary Hotel, Walsall. Back row, left to right: Jim Wood, Chris Mercer and Dennis Armstrong. Front row: Watty Wathen, Mike Haslum, me, John Penn and Tony Hobson – at Keswick in 2001'. (*Jim Shelley*)

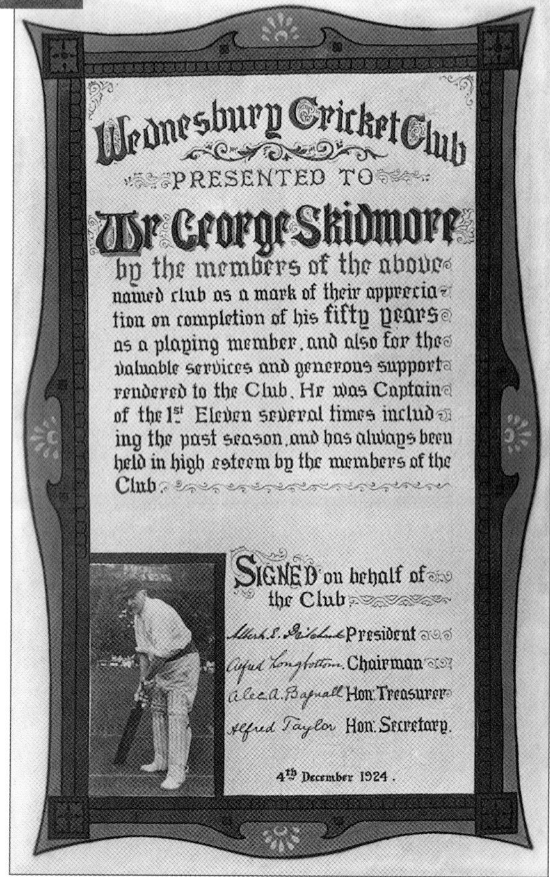

Wednesbury Cricket Club

PRESENTED TO

Mr George Skidmore

by the members of the above named club as a mark of their appreciation on completion of his fifty years as a playing member, and also for the valuable services and generous support rendered to the Club. He was Captain of the 1st Eleven several times including the past season, and has always been held in high esteem by the members of the Club.

SIGNED on behalf of the Club

[illegible] President

Alfred Longbottom Chairman

Alec A. Bagnall Hon: Treasurer

Alfred Taylor Hon: Secretary

4th December 1924.

'My grandfather, George Skidmore, received this appreciation in 1924 for his cricketing prowess.' (*Martin Skidmore*)

'These are my grandfather, George Skidmore, and his son, my father, also George Skidmore, playing cricket at home in Highgate in 1924.' (*Martin Skidmore*)

Mayor John Slater of Walsall. He served as mayor for most of the First World War, despite losing his wife as a result of injuries received from bombs dropped by Zeppelins in 1916. (*D.F. Vodden*)

Ian Payne, who has recently completed a biography of John Stonehouse, says, 'John Stonehouse was Labour MP for Wednesbury from 1957 to 1974, became Minister for Colonies, Aviation and Technology and, in 1968, Postmaster General. In 1976, having been caught in Australia, he was jailed for seven years for theft and false pretences. He had faked his death in 1974 by leaving his clothes on a Miami beach.' (*Ian Payne*)

This is Sergeant Bill Swift, his wife and daughter from my family album. He lived on The Green at Darlaston on the corner of Booth Street.' (*Mrs G. Holmes*)

Arthur Brummell says, 'Billy Tyrell retired from the Level Street Mill Fitters section of Round Oak Steelworks. He originally started in April 1938 as a mill steam engine driver and carried on until the department closed in 1949. When Mr Vern Hill, foreman fitter, presented him with a rocking chair as a leaving present, Bill said he "would now be rocking while they were still rolling!"' (*A. Brummell*)

'A Civic Reception for Flight Lieutenant Webster who was winner of the Schneider Air Race Trophy in 1926. The front row includes William Preston MP, Flight Lieutenant Webster and the mayor, Alderman Joseph Leckie. The chief constable in the back row is C.C.G. Balance.' (*The late Alf Felgate, whose father had been mayor's attendant*)

Geoff Warburton describes this as 'A rare piece of countryside, Saltwells Woods, and my picture includes Mr Westbury walking Ben, 10 June, 1990.' (*Geoff Warburton*)

'This is my uncle, Bert Williams, in the First World War.' (*Mrs Garrington*)

The late Ray Wilcox, pharmacist, said, 'This is the former Trinity Wesleyan church in Corporation Street, Caldmore, Walsall, which was opened in 1876. The spire was blown down in 1894. A new church was built on the site in 1957/8.' The church was packed at Ray Wilcox's funeral on 20 May 2002. (*The late Ray Wilcox's collection*)

ACKNOWLEDGEMENTS

Many people have contributed to this book with both pictures and information, including personal memories: the late Mrs Freda Allen, Mrs Margaret Allen, Dr Geoff Allman, Garry Ashford-Smith, Mr and Mrs Ken Baldwin, Mrs Betty Barratt, Albert Benbow, Geoff Benton, Mr and Mrs Barrie Benton, Mrs Linda Bevan, Mrs Viv Birch (*Express & Star*), Ian Bott, R.A. Brevitt, R. Bristow, Arthur Brummell, Mrs N. Canning, Mrs Deborah Capewell, Keith Cheetham, Rosemary Corns, Ron Davies, Mrs Dennant, Jo Digger, Mrs E. Dwyer, the late J.L. Edwards, Mrs June Ellis, Mr and Mrs Ted Evans, Robert Everton, the late Alf Felgate, E.D. Freeth, Mrs Garrington, Tony Gray, John Griffiths, Eddie Harding, Mrs Mary Harper, Len Harrison, Terry Harrison, Miss Lilian Hawley, Mrs Betty Hemminsley, Ted Hickinbottom, Gordon Hill, Stan Hill, Mrs G. Holmes, John Hubble, Mr K. Hunt, Ken Jeffrey, Carl Kimberley, Ted Knight, Mrs Latham, Mrs Pat Linney, John Llewellyn, Brian Lowe, Rob Madeley, Hon. Miss Anthea Mander, Mrs Kathleen Marklew, Tony Matthews, Mr and Mrs Roy Meller, Mr R. Millward, I. Mitchell, Alan Newman, Peter O'Brien, Fred Parker, Stephen Parkes, Mrs Tina Parton, Don Payne, Ian Payne, Derek Pester, Allan Preston, Ken Proud, the Misses Mary and Nancy Sankey, Dr Eddie Sethna, Bob Shayler, Jim Shelley, Brian Simmonds, Martin Skidmore, Alan Smith MBE, Mrs L. Smithyman, Mrs Souster, Bren Speed, Roy Spencer, Brian Stead, Mrs Mary Stephens, Rex Stone, Roy Taylor, Miss R. Trow, Mrs Barbara Wakelin, Ian Walden OBE, Mrs Marie Ward, Gordon Whiston, Mike Whitehouse, Peter Wilkes, David Wilkins (First House Photography, email: operations@firsthouse.co.uk), Ned Williams, the late Ray Wilcox, Mrs M. Wilde, Peter Wilson, Mrs Margaret Wootton, Peter Wright, Mrs Maureen Vodden. And a very special thanks to my friend Geoff Warburton, who made available his extensive slide collection with much supporting information.

Every effort has been made to contact the owners of copyright of pictures where it did not rest with those who owned the prints.